INTRODUCTION
by
Henny Braund
Chief Executive
Anthony Nolan

I was delighted when Jeni told me that she wanted to donate the proceeds from the sale of her book of beautiful poems to support the work of Anthony Nolan.

Anthony Nolan was established more than forty years ago when a remarkable woman called Shirley Nolan was told that her young son, Anthony, who was suffering from a rare illness of the immune system, would die unless a matching donor could be found to provide him with a bone marrow, or stem cell, transplant.

Shirley was horrified to discover that there was no organised system anywhere in the world for matching potential donors to people with life-threatening illnesses like Anthony's. So she decided to set one up. Anthony Nolan was the world's first stem cell register. It now holds the names of more than half a million potential donors. Thanks to Shirley, today there are twenty-five million people on registers worldwide.

By the time Shirley founded what was then known as the *Anthony Nolan Bone Marrow Trust*, Jeni had already been working as a nurse for more than a decade. It was while she was nursing that she began writing poetry and, as you will discover, many of her poems are inspired by her experiences caring for others. From the premature baby unit in Birmingham to helping those at the end of their lives to die with dignity. She and her young family, all of whom also feature in the following pages, returned to her native Devon, in 1973. Now another generation provides inspiration.

'*Wanted*', in which Jeni's trademark humour and remarkable ability to rhyme are to the fore, is one of my favourites. It succinctly describes what we do at Anthony Nolan and ends with an urgent call to action. Each year in the UK, two thousand people suffering from a range of blood cancers and other conditions urgently require a stem cell transplant. We are still only able to find a matching donor for half of these. And not everyone who finds a donor will survive. We are working to recruit more potential donors to our register and to improve the science around transplantation so that eventually everyone who needs a transplant will find a donor.

I hope you enjoy reading this lovely collection of poems as much as I have. Every copy purchased helps Anthony Nolan add more donors to our register and also supports our crucial research. But we are still some way from achieving our ambition of finding a stem cell donor for everyone who needs a lifesaving transplant. Your support is crucial in helping us achieve that objective, so thank you.

If you'd like to find out about other ways you can help, please visit our website at www.anthonynolan.org.

Heartlands

*For Catherine
Best Wishes.
Jeni Braund*

the poetry of

Jeni Braund

First published 2016
Ottery Writers
Copyright © all poems remain with Jenifer Braund.

ISBN 978-1537077611

All rights reserved. No part of this book may be reproduced or transmitted in any form without prior written consent from the copyright owner with the exception of excerpts for review purposes.

Book Design & Cover: Simon Cornish

Contents

INTRODUCTION	1
ACKNOWLEDGEMENTS	13

Child of The Sea - beginnings

WESTWARD HO!	17
CHILD OF THE SEA	18
WANTED	20
THE TANGLED WEB	22
THE SEA	24
THE MINUTE	26
HARTLAND	27
HARTLAND'S LIGHT	28
TORRINGTON	30
IF I WAS NOT	31
LAKELAND HOLIDAY	32
GRASMERE SPORTS	34
SPRING	36
THE ELM	38
THE OAK TREE AND THE ROSE	40
THE ROSE	41
EXMOUTH DAWN	42
DAWN'S CHORUS	43
QUERULOUS CROWS	44
THE NEWS	46
MAGIC ON THE MOOR	48
MOON POEM	50
GAIA	51
DEVON	52
ANNUAL MIGRATION	53

Mischief Sleeps
– family fun

MISCHIEF SLEEPS	57
THE MUSE	58
DREAMS	59
TOPSY - TURVY	60
PIRATES	61
THE CURL	62
THREE LITTLE CHILDREN	63
DELIGHT	64
MY HOUSE	65
MY SON	66
BROCKWAYS	67
SUMMER	68
MORNING	69
MISSED	70
NOT AGAIN	71
THE HUNTER	72
K 9	73
THE SLUG	74
A SNAIL	75
JOY	76
SERVERS	77
A SPARROW DIED	78
MARK	79
CHRIS	80
CAROLYN	81
CAROLYN'S LONDON	82
HELP	84
PEN BERI HOLIDAY	85
MISSING	86
NIGHT DUTY	88
NIGHT NURSE	89
NOCTURNAL	90
MUM	91
REMEMBER	92
TWENTY-FIRST BIRTHDAY	93

COMING OF AGE	94
MEETINGS	96
FOR SARAH	98
VERA	100
SECOND TIME AROUND	102
HOMAGE TO MICHAEL'S FEET	104
Ps & Qs	106
SPECIES FAECES	108
A POLITICALLY INCORRECT AND DISCRIMINATORY WARNING	110
FEAR	111
7TH DECEMBER 2013	112
ARLO'S POEM	114
ABBY	116
CHRISTMAS	118
MARJORIE	119
THANK YOU	120

There Have Been Certain Moments
– love and life

FOR M & H	123
MOMENTS	124
UNREQUITED LOVE	126
FOUND	127
LOVE'S THORN	128
DOUBT	129
HOPE	130
MORNING	131
FREEDOM OF SPEECH	132
DESIRE	134
DYING	136
ALL MY TOMORROWS	138
CLOUDBIRTH	139
HATE	140
LONGING	141
FROM WIDGERY CROSS	142
MOLLIE	144

THE QUEST	145
SUMMER	146
ACORN	148
SURPRISE	150
THE WOUNDS OF THE WORLD	152
THE BEECH WOOD	153
LOVE'S WHISPER	154
SUBSTITUTION	156
THE QUESTION	157
TOGETHER	158
THE VISIT	159
THE LETTER	160
EVENING	162
TONIGHT	163
OF LOVE AND LIFE	164
FRIENDS	165
SYCHBANT – UCHAF	166
STOLEN HOURS	167
THE HAND OF TIME	168
WINTER	169
SNIPPETS	170

The Seeker
– a spiritual journey

THE SEEKER	173
LIFE	174
THE CEDAR	175
THE CHRISTMAS BABE	176
A CAROL	178
MORNING	179
A HYMN	180
'TIL WE HAVE FACES	182
THE RICH MAN'S DAUGHTER	184
MYSTERY	185
IF	186
THE CHURCH	187
WHAT IS GOD?	188

ICTHOS	189
EASTER	190
MOVING ON	192
THE GIFT	193
FAREWELL	194
SUMMER RETREAT	196
SUMMER RAIN	198
FISH	199
THE YOUNG ONES	200
GENII LOCI	202
THE WORD	204
NIGHT VISION	206
THE RELUCTANT CHRISTIAN	208
CREDO	210
THREE IN ONE	212
POSBURY	214
SHELL COTTAGE	215
A PERSONAL LORDS PRAYER	218
THE CONGREGATION	219
A TIME	220
THE GIFT OF LOVE	221

The Angel Of Death
— nearing the end

STRANGE QUIET DAY	225
THE ANGEL	226
RETIRED	227
ODE TO RETIREMENT	228
DEATH RIDES THE NIGHT TRAIN	230
YOUTH	232
WAR BIRTH	233
LAMENT	234
MY PATIENT	235
THE STAIRWAY OF SURPRISE	236
DEATH	237
TIME	238
ALONE	239

FOR THOSE OF US WHO LOVED HIM	240
THE DREAM	242
ENGLAND'S GRANDMOTHER	243
THE PATH OF LOVE	244
SADNESS	245
HAIKU	246
SEPTICAEMIA	246
ANOTHER	246
WORK IN PROGRESS	247
GRANDMOTHER	248

Afterword

AUTHOR'S NOTE	250

ACKNOWLEDGEMENTS

I would like to thank the following for their help and encouragement.

The Ottery St Mary Writing Group for listening to and critiquing my poems and stories, and for encouraging me to pull it all together and publish.

Particular thanks are due to an amazing proof reading trio of authors, Viv Laine, Serena Cairns, and Eleanor Piper, who wield a ferocious red pen.

To Simon Cornish, author, animator and encourager; who designed both book and cover and led me through a new world with gentle patience. He was encouraging and firm with this undisciplined mind.

Thanks to my son Mark, author and playwright and his wife Henny who brought something very special to our family, and also gave me a purpose to publish.

And of course to all my beautiful family who have been the unwitting inspiration of many of my poems. I have been blessed with many wonderful friends over the course of my life; to those still around, you know who you are. To those who have passed on and who live in my heart. Thank you.

And finally to Dr Rowan Williams, former Archbishop of Canterbury, thank you for your kind words.

CHILD

OF

THE

SEA

beginnings

WESTWARD HO!

More than these others you alone are home,
Where childhood's sweetest fantasy took flight.
When shelter was denied a child and mother,
'Twas you that took them in one moonlit night.

Did you bestow this gift of love, this yearning
Deep in the saddened heart of lonely child,
And know that all your loveliness and caring
Would invade her being, leave her heart beguiled?

That she would come again with love and gladness
And show her children secrets of her own;
Your rocky cliffs which once absorbed her sadness
And turned to joy and giving when full grown.

Your pebbled ridge, your sand hills and bleak burrows,
Each inch familiar, loved, remembered yet,
Beloved cliffs and green clad tors and lookout
Are part of life I never shall forget.

CHILD OF THE SEA

Child of the sea, you wander free
On that fringe of the earth where the land meets the sea.
Nimble your feet over pebble and rock,
With a smudge on your nose and a tear in your frock.

Called by a voice none other can hear,
A faraway look and a heart free from fear.
Alone and apart you explore and you roam
With sublime disregard when it's time to go home.

The rock pools attract you a moment or two
But God's wide Atlantic is calling to you,
Swift as a naiad, you fling off your clothes
And enter wild water with a flash of your toes.

Wildest of elements breaks over your head,
Great foaming breakers could break you instead,
Laughing defiance you plunge and you dive,
This watcher is fearful that you won't survive.

But child of one greater than any on earth,
On crest of great wave as if sea gives you birth,
Streaming and steaming you rise from the tide,
Your laughter rings out as by warm sun you're dried.

Off again wandering, clothes trailing behind,
You slowly remember and dress, then you find
Another loved treasure high up on the cliff.
Higher you scramble while I am scared stiff.

Weary and anxious, I go on my way,
Yet somehow there's comfort in seeing your play,
As if some great mystery watches and guides you-
All-powerful love walks protecting beside you.

WANTED
The Anthony Nolan Poem

Stem cell technology, marrow to share,

What can you offer to show that you care?

It takes not a moment to spit in a pot,

And if you're a match, it can matter a lot.

You spit to register your HLA*

Men, sixteen to thirty, you're wanted today.

Ethnic minorities, Asian and Black

Are desperately needed to lead the attack.

For Anthony Nolan, it all came too late,

The bequest that he left calling all to donate;

For leukaemia sufferers might get a chance,

To fight and recover from cancer's advance.

If chance makes you a hero, a brief hospital visit

To donate your bone marrow, is the simple requisite.

Tissue typed to a patient, you may well discover

You've enabled a dying child to recover.

So why are you waiting, you heros who care?

Your fun filled tomorrows, with a spit you can share.

Be a match, take the test and save someone's tomorrow,

It takes but a moment to save loved ones from sorrow.

*HLA = Human Leucocyte Antigen

THE TANGLED WEB

You gave me life in time of war,
Uncertainty your daily chore.
Times of struggle, times of stress,
With little time for tenderness.

The bonds of friendship as they grew
Brought love, support, a haven too.
The cost of partnership in care
Was the child's love you were forced to share.

No one is owned, nothing belongs-
It's a lesson of life when rights seem wrongs.
To get what we want we struggle and strive
And sometimes regret that we are alive.

The deeper we struggle, the more we deceive,
The tighter the tangled web we weave.
The harder we fight this thing called life,
The greater the stress, the deeper the strife.

But time has a way of healing pain,
Lessens regrets, brings new chances again,
Strengthens old bonds, forges new ties,
Proves us again whether foolish or wise.

THE SEA

I am the sea.
I wash all shores on earth.
I am the sea.
All continents I girth.
I hide a thousand secrets from the land.
I hide uncounted graves, each one unplanned.

I am the sea,
Home to creatures, great and small.
I am the sea.
The whale, the shrimp, my creatures all.
A thousand metres deep my children play,
Each one survives to be another's prey.

I am the sea.
Come splash in my warm waves.
I am the sea.
Forget those ancient graves.
Today I am deceiving, gentle, mild.
Come, mother, trust me with your little child.

I am the sea,
Whipped up by wind and storms.
I am the sea.
Unleashed, the fury of my wildest forms
Gave birth to earth's first life, and, at her end,
I'll lap her wounded shores, her one true friend.

THE MINUTE

I'm not quite sure just what I feel,
It's rather like-
I'm not quite real.
I must be in a sorry state,
And yet it's one
I cannot hate,
For, if I hate the way I feel,
I think I might
Not feel quite real.

HARTLAND

Proud headland jutting out into great ocean,
Stark backdrop to a wild and raging sea,
Your green and golden fields in constant motion
And at your feet, quaint cobbled Clovelly.

I've watched a setting sun paint you with shadows.
In scarlet mantle you have met the night.
I've seen you girded shyly as the mist rose
And all but hid your powerful warning light.

I've walked your beach in gentle summer sunshine.
I've climbed your cliffs, explored your caves anew.
I've seen your raging seas destroy a lifeline
And mercilessly break a ship in two.

Yet you'll stand firm when I am long forgotten,
When other men will come and till your soil.
As in the past, great men will dream about you,
Majestic grandeur watching o'er their toil.

HARTLAND'S LIGHT

Anger tore the blinkers from his eyes.
He walked the rocky cliffs 'neath sullen skies.
The battlemented clouds swirled all around,
Beneath him raging seas tore at the ground.
Below, the bouldered bay was lashed with foam,
White horses filled the caves of childhood's home.
Remembered days of freedom and of joy,
A childhood's wild adventuring; each ploy
Excitement to a seaman's boy.

Blinded by the stinging salt-filled air
He saw her in his mind's eye resting there,
Admired the laughing eyes, the dimpled cheek,
The invitation in them bid him seek
His happiness beside her; in her arms
Ecstatic love would mellow life's alarms.
The rain-soaked cloak slapped wickedly his face,
Brought caution to his wandering mind's disgrace,
Adulthood mindful of this dangerous place.

A piercing shaft of moonlight from the skies
    Lit up the sea the colour of her eyes.
Soft-spoken words of love had filled his life,
    Until he found she was another's wife.
    Blinded by his love, he blundered on,
    Struggling to believe that she was gone.
    And then tonight, a cheery note farewell.
He crossed the gale-torn cliffs deep in his hell
    A distant thunderclap a warning bell.

    Beaten by the raging wind and storm,
A need for human kindness dry and warm,
Turned his unthinking footsteps to the beach,
'Cross boulders wet and slippery, beyond reach
of human foot. Heaven remembered childhood's pledge
And guided thoughtless footsteps 'cross the ledge;
    Unaware of God's attention, or his plight,
    Numb and cold he strode into the night
Toward the friendly warmth of Hartland's light.

TORRINGTON

Strange little town that sits upon its hilltop,
Surveying proudly valleys far below,
The River Torridge wending through green woodland
Like ancient moat protecting you from foe.

Tall pavement seemed to child a giant's doorstep,
Old Market Square where all who came could meet.
Small friendly inn with crackling log fire blazing
And, best-remembered, May Fair's annual treat.

IF I WAS NOT
A Riddle

'If I was not',
dark nights,
still seas,
no sparkling frosts,
or night-time shadowed trees.

'If I was not',
no hunter's light,
or owl's haunting flight,
or silver path across a darkened sea.

'If I was not',
the weeks would cease to be,
and months' redundancy
would change the shape of years..
and time would cease to be-

What am I?

LAKELAND HOLIDAY

Face to face with splendour,
God's earth in majesty,
For surely here is heaven
And man's own destiny.
The glory of this Lakeland,
Of soaring rampant fell,
Of mere and tarn and sparkling beck
And still and silent well.

The Romans came and conquered-
Long gone in history-
They left an ancient legacy
For modern man to see.
Departed, now their might and strength
Remains within us still,
And those who live amongst it
Give to those who seek their fill.

Yearly we return here,

As the swift from southern shores,

To refresh our souls with stillness,

Bodies freed from daily chores.

And He, in all His caring,

Gave this heaven that we might see

A glimpse of paradise to come,

When we shall all be free.

GRASMERE SPORTS

Grasmere sports- all the fun of the fair-
The world and his wife and their children were there.
Crowds throng the benches and crowds throng the ring,
Each of them wanting to show off their thing,
Prowess at wrestling or running the fell,
The men and the boys, they're bred tough, you can tell.
The man on the speaker has done it for years,
From the crowd he draws laughter; from some he draws tears!

Around us, like bastions, the mountainsides tower,
Thunderheads gather, threat more than a shower,
Yet still the arena is flooded with sun,
Watched over by someone enjoying the fun.
Forgotten the horrors on last nights TV,
For people are gathered in brief harmony.
Bright martial music floats on the breeze-
The band of the 'Borderers' playing to please.

The Cumberland wrestlers all dressed for the kill,
Boys, seven to seventy, race up the hill.
The starting man's pistol gives Jimmy a fright,
The pole-vaulters leap to a staggering height.
'Oh dear! A catastrophe, what shall we do?
The vaulter has broken his pole right in two.'
Beyond the arena, the bright carousel
Amuses the children and Granny as well.

Come the end of the day, all the races are run,
The laurels awarded, the prizes are won.
Competitors vanish to joy or to sorrow,
Back to an everyday world on the morrow.
Spectators disperse, leave their litter behind,
The last missing infant his mother will find.
Grasmere returns to its peace and its quiet,
With a sigh of relief after its annual riot.

SPRING

What happened to March, that the lion's roar
we never did hear this year?
With the lambs it came softly;
with early buds, and a tread that was hard to hear.

Tempting the daffodils out of their shells,
until they were in full bloom.
Then suddenly in swept April,
with almost a sonic boom.

With swirling snow and hailstorms,
and gales that wrecked ships at sea,
Causing the children leaving school,
to a place of safety to flee.

Then the mighty storm clouds sailed
away, and left us a watery sun,
And the shattered and battered mantle of spring,
was back where it begun.

The birds and blooms lifted sodden heads,
to dry in the warmth of the day;
And the children's laughter, bright ever after,
made April showers their play.

THE ELM

Ivy clad skeletons, fingering the sky-
Rows of gracious elm trees, naked to the eye,
Stark against the skyline, outlined by setting sun.
Nature has decided that their days on earth are done.

For once mankind's not guilty of negligence or rape,
With ravages of beetles, little hope of late escape.
Perhaps it's a reminder of nature's mighty power?
Mankind is but a fleeting thing, a passing summer shower.

And I, who mourn their passing, such glory as was ours,
I walked beneath the cooling shade amid soft scented flowers,
And never thought the day would come the mighty elm would die,
Make its final disappearance from our English country sky.

What sin has it committed to forfeit with its life,
To be cut down and burned to ash with tree-man's saw and knife?
Is there perhaps a lesson here from some celestial source?
Must we destroy our countryside before man shows remorse?

We push out ever further with our 'dark satanic mills'
And scar this beauteous country with man's logic and his ills.
Remember now, the stately elm its nemesis has met.
Wake up mankind! Be cautious, just, less we our end regret.

THE OAK TREE AND THE ROSE

At the bottom of my garden stand an oak tree and a rose.
Since we came, they've been entwined there in an intimate repose.

The oak has weathered winter storms of fifty years or more.
Each year it is refurbished new from nature's springtime store.

It waits its rose companion's bloom, encircled in embrace.
At last her climbing tendrils flower; her perfume lends him grace.

They complement each other from spring until September.
The scarlet hip in autumn gleams through acorn's golden ember.

The squirrels hunt frenetically for autumn's harvest gifts.
October mists, November frosts, bring golden leaves in drifts.

Tenaciously, the rose clings tight as winter storm rain lashes.
The oak withstands the blast; its roots dig deep as thunder crashes.

Through winter's hibernation the companion's saps diminish.
The briar-encircled skeleton stands gaunt 'til winter's finish.

As longer daylight hours proclaim the warmer months to come
In flaming hues of sunset, the oak and rose are one.

THE ROSE

Perfection for a day, so soft the silken petals of the rose echo the seasons of the year.

Where does its life begin? Where does it end?

From barren twigs the swelling bud bursts forth,
Each leaf unfurls to meet the warming sun.

The budding flower emboldened by spring's warmth shows a touch of colour,

Blushing softly, lifting its face to the caress of its lover, the sun.

Swift that caress, as sunset fades, leaving the silver moon to steal its glory with a kiss.

And, after that perfect day, the morning dew leaves tears upon the fullness of the rose.

As autumn surely comes, the petals once like silk, curl back, fade, fall.

Youth has gone, yet beauty lingers on, in memory the scent of yesterday is barely lost;

before the beauty of the berry, tells the story of the passing seasons.

EXMOUTH DAWN

One morn I got up early
And walked down to the sea.
I was the only stranger there,
No seabird noticed me.

A gentle sea lapped golden shore,
A distant cormorant dived
And, deep beyond the misty bar,
An oystercatcher cried.

Without sound the silver mist
Softly began to blush
And wisps and streaks of fleecy cloud
Were touched by artist's brush.

I stood entranced and watched with awe
As light crept o'er the sea,
A misty orb slid into view
With silent majesty.

I watched, with bated reverent breath,
The glorious dawn unfold
And, there before my very eyes,
The world was turned to gold.

DAWN'S CHORUS

Distant hilltops floating
Like islands in the sea.
Beneath the mist, a city sleeps
And plans its destiny.

And in the scattered valleys,
The farmers swiftly rise,
Casting anxious skyward looks
At thunder headed skies.

Alone upon a hilltop,
An artist, with his brush,
Prepares his canvas, chooses paint
And waits for dawn's first blush.

And then outside my window
Morn's early riser cries
And, like musicians tuning up,
Dawn's chorus fills the skies.

QUERULOUS CROWS

Querulous crows, crashing at my window,
Why do you wake me before the sun gets up?
No mating game or rival to see
In the reflection of my glass,
No spring ritual either. For nine months now
You batter and bruise yourselves, leaving
Feathers, blood and dust in your frenzy,
You'll dim your wits with this strange performance.
Querulous crows.

And sometimes, later in the day, you knock
At my French windows, demanding what? Entrance?
The sun is autumn low and winter looms.
A week of grey skies subdue the window's glare,
But the pair of you perch in the trees beside the house and dive.
Is it a game you play? For you seem to take it in turns
cawing encouragement, each to the other.
You have dimmed your wits with this strange performance.
Querulous crows.

What is it you are trying to tell me?
Move on, move out, it's time to change, move, move.
Another family wants this family home and yours is gone!
Is that the message? I'm too slow to know.
You'll have to speak clearer, for my 'crow' is poor.
I looked you up; 'a harbinger of change', 'a messenger',
'a link between here and the world of spirit'.
Is it my wits that are dimmed?
Querulous crows

So now I try to listen, and understand,
the thumps and tappings of your morning visits.
When I peep out, you fly away. Stay and help me understand.
For if I do, maybe you too will be free
of the frenzied need to crash and bang.
Your bruises will heal, your headaches will cease,
Your wits may recover. And I? I will have peace!
Querulous crows!

THE NEWS

Expressionless, the face pours forth the news
To viewers desensitised by too much gore.
Once it used to titillate each sense, the trials of unknown others,
Now, a surfeit of horror numbs all but the most hardened.
The camera's probing eye zooms in on bloodiest scene-
Flies mock the sightless, battered dead.
Awkward limbs rest in technicolour blood.
Who needs a censored Hollywood?
We have the News.

We hung the island map, a cheerful souvenir,
Laughed, for it looks just like a legless goose.
Traced with sure fingers contoured heights we'd walked.
Mountain of Hope they called it, our Mount Teide,
burial place of many an English Lady.
Now I stare and see, instead of contoured lines,
Broken spruce and torn up pines,
Bruised earth and scorched and jagged grooves.
We saw the News.

I swiftly feel the laughter in the cabin,
The first glimpse from the windows of
An island jewel set in a sapphire sea,

Softly wrapped in snow-white cotton clouds,
Emerald and gold bathed in the sun's caress.
The squeal, excited children can't suppress,
Then lost from sight, we dip into soft clouds,
Slender stewardess moves swiftly to her post,
Each charge safely strapped in,
Another routine charter nearly done.
We heard the News at One.

A vivid scene and helplessly I watch,
From some point way above the Captain's head.
Two men, hands, eyes and brains in perfect unison.
I knew before they saw the warning light,
Heard the indrawn breath, the murmured 'Christ.'
All had been well; the beacon marked, approach acknowledged,
The static voice, 'Hold at 5000.' Nothing wrong with that. Then,
'What's that bloody mountain doing there?'
A question frozen on the lips,
As hand and brain and sinew force shrieking metal to respond.
Too late. I saw the News at Eight.

Gazed into the winter fire, watched tongues of flame
Lick round the splintered logs.
Felt his brief, puzzled agony, and wept.

25/4/80 Dan air flight 2008 crashed in Tenerife

MAGIC ON THE MOOR

There's magic in the air tonight,
The crowds are gone and dimmed the lights,
Tonight's performance packed away,
Tomorrow night, another play.

In to the bar, the cast and crew
Relax, the volunteers too,
Post mortem's done, they've had their fun,
Now time for home for old and young.

Tomorrow brings another day,
And back to Sterts you'll make your way,
It all depends on your goodwill,
As Ewart's dream you all fulfil.

When you are gone, the night is stilled
This special place with magic's filled,
And quiet descends and I am left
A tearful eye, a touch bereft.

What is it in this special place,
that draws us all in its embrace?
We manufacture dreams it's true,
And here perform those dreams for you.

MOON POEM

How did it get there, the ball in the sky?
Who do you think could have kicked it so high?
What were they doing and where did they go
And when did it happen? Does anyone know?
I wish you could tell me, I want to know why,
Just who could have kicked it so high in the sky?

GAIA

From up above, or is it from below,
Or from beyond I watch the earth drift so.
Lapis lazuli blue and cotton white-
I even make the day turn into night.

A distant globe that sails an endless deep,
While unaware her teeming billions sleep,
Yet others wake and work and sow and reap,
Some scheme, and steal, and fight, where evils creep.

Where putrid minds exist in furtive light,
And greedy nations seek power and fight,
When children starve and innocents are slain,
Diseases ravage man and droughts the plain.

Millennia pass before her wounds will heal,
And healing sun and soothing rains assuage.
Gaia turns on her diurnal passage,
Driven by a power unknown, unseen,
That keeps her spinning some eternal dream.

DEVON

Devon wears her summer mantle,
Patchwork quilt of green and gold.
Hills and valleys, rock-strewn beaches—
Peace and glory to behold.

ANNUAL MIGRATION

From coast to coast, from moor to shore,
From ancient walls to village greens,
Here we are blessed to work and live
In summer's warmth and winter's chill;
We welcome you, who travel far,
To take your rest, free from the stress,
Of city lives.
May your distress be blessed with ease
And when you leave, may we suggest
A swift return to Devon, please?

MISCHIEF SLEEPS

family fun

MISCHIEF SLEEPS

My child of three asleep in bed,
A golden halo round his head,
And one next door, a boy of four.
How mischief sleeps. And now one more.
'Dear Lord, this one within make gentle,
Another boy will drive me mental.
A golden girl with curly hair
And eyes of blue and skin so fair.'
This prayer I prayed six years ago.
I must have been dim-witted, slow.
A darling daughter have I, true-
A minx, a demon, tomboy too,
More trouble than her brothers sure,
'Dear Lord, I beg of you, no more'!

THE MUSE

I yearn to write, this urge in me frustrated.
A tolerant smile from sceptic husband dear.
Then suddenly it comes, the new beginning
And from outside a crash, a howl, a tear.

Dear heaven, this motherhood bestowed upon me
Is loved and cherished, but I beg as well
A little patience, peace and inspiration.
I can do it if they'd only go to h***!

DREAMS

Strange to think my childhood dreams
Were dreamt by those before me,
Kipling, Kingsley, Grenville bold,
Who sailed the seas for Spanish gold
And kept the shores of England free.

Brave deeds those men of England wrought,
Who loved and dreamed before me,
Whose poetry and truth foretold
The mighty wars both real and cold
And saved this childhood for me.

TOPSY - TURVY

Roses in December,
Winter snow in May.
Life seems topsy-turvy,
Nothing's right today.

One race fights for freedom,
Another's overrun.
Life is one long battle,
Has the last war begun?

PIRATES

I stood on the pebble ridge, gazed out to sea,
Mindful of those who shape man's destiny.
Did they also stand dreaming and long for adventure,
Drawn by the beckoning call of the sea,
Stirred by the wheeling and cries of the seabirds,
Drawn from the safety of Devon's green lea?
My little pirate's a child on gold beaches,
Hers, an explorer across distant seas.
He must have been lured by the tales of adventure,
Heard from the sailors by Devon's wild seas.

THE CURL

Lonely was a golden curl
Upon slender nape of little girl.
She paused entranced as fine strands fell
And tickled softly nose of Nell.
She blew and watched them drift away,
Then wondered what would mother say.
A guilty glance, a tube of glue,
A horrid mess, 'My, look at you!'
Reproach, a scold, a tearful girl
With but a lonely little curl.

THREE LITTLE CHILDREN

Three little children home from school,
One had measles, two had flu.
All ate oranges, pips and all,
All sprouted orange trees six feet tall.
Branches grew from ears and toes,
Green leaves sprung from eyes and nose.
Two grew oranges, one grew pears,
They picked the fruit as they climbed the stairs.
When the doctor called to see the sight,
She thought a gardener would be more right.
They picked the fruit and ate it all,
Then the leaves began to fall.
The moral of this story is -
Don't eat too many oranges!

DELIGHT

The small child watched in wonder
The antics of the bee
As it flew from honeysuckle
To the heights of yonder tree.
Her freckled snub nose buried
In the flower to smell and see,
A lift of golden head, a grin,
'That flower tickled me'.

MY HOUSE

The lane that leads to my house
Is the turning on the right.
You pass through leafy tunnel
If you venture out at night.

And in the deep midwinter,
When Jack Frost has been around,
The branches turn to sparkling ice
With diamonds on the ground,
The hedge a silver filigree
Of spiders' fine-spun lace,
All sparkles in the moonlight
In this lovely fairy place.

In warmer months, when Spring comes
And the air with scent is filled,
Alternate trees of pink and gold
Some long gone gardener willed,
That in this place of loveliness
Tired travellers would rest
And find some sweet contentment
In life's never ending quest.

MY SON

The room is white
And in the night,
Attendants gowned and clever.
The mother moans,
The doctor groans,
'Lord, we'll be here forever'.

The silence breaks,
The ceiling swims,
The mystery unfolds,
And in that harsh and clinic light,
The doctors and the nurses fight;.
My private miracle is born
My son cries greeting to the dawn.

BROCKWAYS

The spirit of Brockways haunts me still,
It peoples my mind and it always will,
With words of wonder and words of joy
When scent of blossom my senses cloy.

When it's time to wander away from my home
To that greater adventure where I may roam,
Where the good Lord waits in eternity
And the soul of a poet at last can be free.

SUMMER

Lazy summer sunshine,
Drifting wisps of hay,
Gardens filled with laughter
Of children as they play.

Drowsy cows a-munching
The golden fields of hay,
People wandering freely
On a perfect summer's day.

Blackbird sings with fervour,
Sparrows search for food,
Encouraging the youngsters
To fly and leave the brood.

Lazily I gather
Nature's treasures from the lane
To take home and remember
When the autumn brings the rain.

MORNING

A stillness in the valley,
A city in the mist.
The countryside wakes slowly,
The hills are first sun-kissed,
Sleepy eyed and warm inside,
I watch the world awaken,
Then other thoughts invade my mind
With smells of eggs and bacon.

MISSED

I leaned from the window and listened to the hush.
I heard a little scurry, then a noisy padding rush.
I caught a glimpse of ginger fur, a stealthy creeping glide,
A shiver ran down over me. I'm glad I was inside.

Silence fell, the garden stilled, a distant donkey brayed.
I heard a sudden piercing shriek, I knew it was afraid;
I couldn't see, except inside, that frightened furry scrap,
But felt his terror, frozen like a lightning thunderclap.

A sudden movement in the trees the cat's attention drew,
The mouse, released from stupor ran, as black-bird skyways flew.
The trap was sprung, the cat attacked, too late its prey had fled—
And sleepy eyed but filled with joy, I tumbled back to bed.

NOT AGAIN

Oh kitten new, why always do
You climb the highest tree?
You know I cannot climb like you,
Or bear your frightened plea.

Now I must summon, drat you cat,
Some courage and a ladder.
Whenever you get stuck like that,
I'm mad and getting madder.

Now teetering, nervous, feeling weird,
I reach the top, and you?
You, little pest, have disappeared,
And I am left to stew.

THE HUNTER

He sniffs
    Around
        A mouse
            He's found
                He sniffs
                    He smells
                        A mouse
                            He fells

It runs
    He stalks
        His claws
            Like pins
                Flash swiftly
                    As
                        His meal
                            He wins.

K 9

Wogga the dogga was pretty not plain,
As she frisked through the cowslips and ran down the lane.
Of sheep she was wary, of cows plain afraid,
Though deep in her dreams, lots of dragons she slayed.

She barked at the postman, she snarled at the cat,
But ran away frightened when I shook the mat.
A coward at heart but a guard dog when roused-
If she gets much bigger, we may be rehoused.

THE SLUG

I am a slug
Who was found on a rug
By a lady who thought me a bug.
I was flushed down the loo,
Disinfected with Bloo,
Now I'm a blue-blooded slug.

A SNAIL

A snail in full sail,
Feeling terribly pale,
Fell into a glass of beer,
His wife cried, 'You 'oughter
Fall into some water
And wash all that ale off you'.

He pulled in his horns
When he trod on her corns
And climbed up the garden wall.
She threatened and grumbled,
'Til he nigh on well tumbled
And had him a nasty great fall!

JOY

Joy be thankful,
Joy be gay,
The washing and ironing's
done today.

Joy be thankful,
Joy be quick,
Granny fell over
Her walking stick.

Joy by name,
By nature too.
What is the next line?
I haven't a clue.

SERVERS

Children's faces shining bright,
Softly lit by candlelight.
Yours to serve and yours to own,
Shall they remember when they're grown?

A SPARROW DIED

Today a sparrow died.
Injured and bleeding, it lay upon my hand.

It flew into the window.
My son, distressed, hurried for my help.

Saddened, he turned away, his burden lifted.
I took its weight; what else are mothers for?

The creature flutters blindly.
I feel the racing heart, the dumb appeal.

It bleeds, concussed.
I know again the helplessness of death.

MARK

Wake up, wake up, fourteen year old,
The day is bright and sunny.
The post and gifts will come tonight,
You may get lots of money.

Wake up, wake up, get out of bed,
Today you may go far
And if you beat Dad playing golf,
He'll take you to the bar.

He'll buy you lemonade and lime
Until you're fit to burst,
Until old Harry says it's time,
Or 'til you've quenched your thirst.

So Happy Birthday M A B
And have a happy day,
And if it's fish and chips for tea
Perhaps you'd like to pay?

CHRIS

Congratulations, teenager,
Thirteen years old at last.
You're growing up, I'll wager
Childhood's never flown so fast.

I hope the things you've wanted
Will always come your way,
And we've tried hard to find the things
You wanted for today.

We've tried to be the friends you need,
Though parents seldom are.
We've tried to give you happiness,
Knowing one day you'll go far.

And when you go, we hope you know
We've loved you good and bad.
Through all your ups and downs, we'll be
Your loving Mum and Dad.

CAROLYN

My daughter of ten has arrived home from school,
Full of excitement and damp from the pool.
'Please write me a poem, it must have ten lines
Just write about anything, gardens or wines!
I'll do my best writing and send it away.
If I win a prize, 'twill mean no school one day.
Get on with it Mum, you can do it, I know.'
Then why is it just at the moment I'm slow?
My muse has deserted, inspiration has fled,
And ten year old daughter is tucked up in bed!

CAROLYN'S LONDON

Carolyn went to London, the family went too.
There was brother Mark and brother Chris and cousin Sara Sue.
They drove along the motorway until they reached the end.
Daddy put the brakes on at a rather nasty bend.

They parked the car so neatly at a most convenient spot,
Or so said mum to daddy, but the traffic cop said not.
At last they found a parking place and started to explore.
Among so many foreign folk, they met the man next door.

They walked down Piccadilly, dragging mum past all the shops.
Dad almost had his pocket picked and nearly called the cops.
They all stared up at Nelson, who surveyed Trafalgar Square.
They climbed up on the lions, who returned a baleful stare.

Cousin Sara fed the pigeons, then they walked down to Whitehall.
They tried to make the Horse Guards laugh, then Carolyn had a fall.
They looked at Winston Churchill, who was really rather large,
Then suddenly they saw the Queen with Royal entourage.

The Palace of Westminster is really rather vast;
By the time they'd seen the Abbey dinnertime was flying past.
They sat on the embankment to eat their picnic lunch,
Interrupted by a pigeon who insisted on a munch.

A trip upon a riverboat came next to see Tower Bridge.
They queued to see the Royal Jewels and their ancient heritage.
The Beefeaters were handsome in their scarlet, black and gold.
They said they locked up children who didn't do as they were told.

They walked back through the city, which was rather old and glum,
And saw the Bank of England. 'That's the Corn Exchange,' said mum.
At last they came upon St Paul's and rested on the steps.
They saw an old and dirty tramp and cousin Sara wept.

Mum said, 'Why are you crying,' when Carolyn started too.
'It's for all the dirty people and the sick and lonely too.'
They went in the cathedral and quietly said a prayer;
Dad said it was the thing to do for people in despair.

And when they came outside again, the tramp he smiled at mum
And two little golden headed girls, who were walking in the sun.
And when at last they headed home, tired out but full of joy.
They all agreed that London's great, but dad just said 'Oh boy!'

HELP

One little office in a sleepy Devon town-
A micro-computer spills its print upon the ground.
Demented operator seeks a cursor flying past,
With VDU and 'floppy discs', it's all a bit too fast.

To learn computer language, whether 'basic' or 'adds plus',
It's just a little difficult, a bit confused, that's us.
The boss, he won't be beaten, he's an awkward sort of cuss,
While up country with the 'mainframe',
They can't understand the fuss.

They say it's all so easy; wish they'd come and show us how.
The client's not a patient man, he wants his figures now!
The boss is working weekends and he keeps us here 'til six.
I wish he'd take a month off with his 'micro' box of tricks.

PEN BERI HOLIDAY

Thank you for this place of peace and beauty,
For sun-filled days and thunder-headed skies,

For stonechats scolding, falcons' silent soaring,
Pen Beri crag and every flower-filled rise.

Knowing that such promises are broken,
Let me return one day before too long,

And find again the welcome in this hillside-
Peace for the soul and, for the heart, a song.

Thanks, too, for the welcome of flowers in every room,
And every creature comfort, the days have passed too soon.

MISSING

I stepped into the frozen night in search of you,
The icy blood coursed silent in my veins.
Alone he has returned your favourite stallion,
But yours were not the hands that held his reins.

Foam flecked, head hung, and gallant flanks still heaving,
I mounted him, for he knows were you are,
And, by the glow of silent silver moonlight,
We search the snowbound moor; we canter far.

So bitter is the night, I ride in stupor.
My eyes with fearful tears for you are blind,
The hands that hold his reins are stilled by terror,
And you, a frozen shadow on my mind.

He stumbles weary, I awake from numbness
As fingers cold and stiff collect the reins.
Dulled senses find that we have left the moorland,
His tired hooves now clatter down strange lanes.

In icy mist, a faint glow grows before us.
Tired stallion carries me into the gloom,
Beyond the yard, a friendly door is opened,
Warm faces draw me to a firelit room.

With love and thankful prayer, I kneel beside you,
And thank the kindly folk that took you in,
And with acclaim, tell of the faithful stallion
Whose courage had alone the will to win.

We turn outside to give him food and shelter,
To thank our faithful friend and stroke proud head,
To share with him our love for ever after
But, strength exhausted, faithful mount is dead.

NIGHT DUTY

Nurse, Nurse!
Your feet you curse,
And hold your aching back.
You fall asleep,
Still on your feet.
The mood you're in is black.

Nurse, Nurse,
A patient calls.
Sore feet and back are gone.
A ministering angel
Dressed in white,
'God bless you when I'm gone.'

NIGHT NURSE

The night was still, a child cried.
Young girl in white is by her side.
Soft, soothing comfort soon bestowed,
Too young herself for motherhood,
Her touch is sure, her instinct good.
The night nurse tiptoes round the ward,
Young patients sleep safe, reassured.

NOCTURNAL

Why are you marching, marines in fatigues?
You shout when the night nurse is sleeping.
Left Right, Left Right,
When softly your boots should be creeping.

You train for a war where controversy reigns;
She rests for a war that's eternal.
Left Right, Left Right,
Go softly, her day is nocturnal.

Your youth assaults courses, learns weaponry skills,
Her skills soothe diseases and weeping.
Left Right, Left Right.
March softly, the night nurse is sleeping.

MUM

If you said you were twenty, they'd know you were kidding.
If you said you were thirty, 'Like hell!'

If you said you were forty, they'd say you were naughty,
And likewise with fifty as well.

If you said you were sixty, 'Just right for your age',
And where are the laurels in that?

But admit that you're seventy, sit back with a smile,
And bask in the looks of surprise for a while.

Relax in the splendour and glory of fame,
Enjoy your good fortune and keep your good name.

PS
And now that you're eighty, the poem must grow-
Is it all still a secret or can everyone know?

REMEMBER

Remember her loveliness,
Remember her youth,
Remember her playfulness,
Remember her truth,

Remember her teenager dreams and ideas,
Remember her longings, her hopes and her fears,
Remember depression and anger and tears,
Remember the joy that she gave through the years.

Remember anxiety, doubting and fuss,
Remember the feelings engendered in us!
Remember her first love, her pony, her bike,
Remember her late nights with Martin and Mike,

With Lalo, with Kelvin, with Nick and with Paul,
Oh yes, there were girls, Claire, Jackie and all.
She leaves us to take up a life of her own,
We watch her with pride, this our daughter full grown.

Remember her childhood,
Remember her grace,
Remember her gentleness,
Remember her face.

TWENTY-FIRST BIRTHDAY

In life's uncertain moments
Never lose sight of your dreams.
Always believe in the rainbow,
However elusive it seems.

Whenever you're feeling lonely
Reach out with a friendly smile.
'Laugh and the world laughs with you'
Is a maxim still worthwhile.

When love seems a long time coming
Remember the best is rare.
It may take the summer of life to grow,
So nurture it with care.

Though you travel the wide world over,
Love will be waiting for you.
The day that you find your rainbow,
Is the day that dreams come true.

COMING OF AGE

Coming of age at eighteen was
                freeing you from your youth.
Letting go as best we could,
                watching you find your truth.
Coming of age at twenty-one
                is freeing you from our past,
Encouraging you to be yourself,
                in spite of all doubt cast.

Remembering that times have changed
                and our ways are not yours,
That the sum of our experiences
                can never smooth your course;
'Loving you' cannot hold you back,
                yet 'loving you' can't help knowing
The emptiness when you are gone,
                that 'loving you' can't help showing.

Yet always your life will be our life,
                in the news and laughter you share;
Children are ours for such a brief span
                - motherhood's a lifetime care

A child who becomes a parent sees
        a new perspective on life,
Awareness that grows as experience
        shows that love lasts longer than life.

We say goodbye with much sorrow,
        yet pride takes first place in our heart.
We hope for a joyful tomorrow,
        as endless tomorrows will start.
A future that's full of unknowing will
        bring out your doubts and your fears.
It's natural that every beginning is
        christened by anguish and tears.

If all were as certain as knowing,
        no adventure would ever befall.
There'd be no point in struggle and striving;
        there'd be no point in living at all.
So face your tomorrow with courage,
        grasp each opportunity strong.
With friendship and love, guardian angel above,
        may your new life be joyful and long.

MEETINGS

I have just met the father of my grandchildren,
Laughing brown eyes in strong compassionate face.
We are yet to call each other 'son', 'mum', but that will come.
Stressful necessity evoked by the power of love-
This meeting of the packaging.

Ocean and continent separate loving generations.
'The world is yours' I laughingly challenged
the teenager seeking herself;
Only to weep when the search began.
Emotional meetings,
Joyful greetings,
Tearful goodbyes - a return
To distant lives, already planning another visit.

Then recently, a call out of time:
'I think I'm in love, I wanted to share it with you.'
Breathless laughter,
Hesitant joy,
Parental questions.

An airport greeting, hugs and laughter, searching eyes,
Watching lovers play, kisses, whispers,
Secret glances; messages of love.
Unspoken questions answered.

Had I forgotten the urgency of love,
The value of every precious moment,
The need to share entwined with the need to be alone?

There, in the depth of mind, the scars unzip,
My own vulnerability fired by the raw energy of love.
Tormented by a need to be a part of love,
Held back by their need for lovers' proofs.

I tremble, turn away lest too much shows,
Aware of stumbling emotions seeking a place within the whole.

I have just met the father of my grandchildren.
The rest will come.

FOR SARAH

There's a silver moon just hanging
In an English evening sky.
It's nice to know that same old moon
Shines down on you and I.

Five times a thousand miles away
From here I'd like to be,
Especially on your birthday
For a hug from you to me.

So here's a special silver chain
To stretch from me to you,
And every year, come shine or rain,
I'll send a charm to you.

And when you're twenty-one, let's count.
Your chain will crowded be
With fifteen or more memories
Of times that used to be.

By then I'll be a mommy too,
With kids like Mitch and Meg and you,
And you can come and visit me
And tell my kids what they should do.

I miss you more than I can tell,
And all my Kansas family too,
But all being well, before the Fall
I'll be coming home to you.

VERA

Eighty years old on St. Patrick's Day,
An ache in her heart and a hair or two grey,
Always a smile and a sandwich and tea,
One of earth's angels, that's our little Vee.

The best of good neighbours, the dearest of friends,
Whatever the problem, a kind ear she lends.
The rent girl on Friday a refuge will find,
The neighbourhood doggies all know she is kind.

Always a biscuit, a pat on the head,
They all know her routine, they all know her tread.
With bread for the magpies and crumbs for 'Joe Crow',
Four walks a day to her cheeks bring a glow.

The years we have loved her stretch into the past,
The love she has given is returned and will last.
With friends and with family to share in her day,
Some will come calling, and some miles away

Will be thinking about her on her special day.
Glad that they've known her and touched by her way.
All of us wish that the years still to come
Will be happy and healthy and filled with her fun.

SECOND TIME AROUND

Remember when she made a life of her own-
She went to America, our daughter full-grown.
Now her turn is come for heart-rending farewell,
As the son she has cherished leaves home for a spell.

With high school behind him and laurels well won,
He seeks higher honours, his place in the sun.
To earn it, his will he'll submit to the Chain
of Command, in the military place of acclaim.

A plebe in the first year, the lowest of all,
He'll be tested and tried, 'til he yields to the call.
He'll wonder what hit him, this free-chosen course.
The dream of his youth may yet bring remorse.

Yet, at Westpoint, he'll learn to depend on his team,
At 'cadre's' command, he will learn not to scream,
By submitting to orders that oft' don't make sense,
Belittled, demeaned, he must not take offence.

Tired to exhaustion, he's pummelled and drilled,
'Til too weary to question, obedience instilled.
One day he'll make sense of the choices he made,
Whether army or civvy, the game he'll have played.

The fact he survived in that toughest regime,
Will one day bring blessings, at present unseen;
Whatever he chooses we'll proud of him be,
Our young man in love with the land of the free.

HOMAGE TO MICHAEL'S FEET

They'll traverse hallowed halls,
They'll scale high walls.
At cadre's shout, they'll wheel about,
The training Plain in sun and rain,
And proudly bear your weight through Westpoint Gate.

Grey eyes survey, grey walls surround,
Six feet below, companions found,
Two feet, ten toes, you fall, we'll rest,
At heart and sinew's quest, we'll rise once more,
Support your weight through Westpoint Gate.

As Buckner does its worst, sore feet and blisters burst,
Through shake and shiver, through the river,
Quake and quiver 'neath the wire, muscles weary,
vision bleary, nerves on fire,
We'll share your fate, we'll bear your weight,
and march you back through Westpoint Gate.

You enter now in trust and truth,
One of a thousand willing youth.
In six weeks time, you'll join the feast
With head held high; you've slain the beast!
They'll watch with pride those feet parade,
We'll proudly bear your weight
through Westpoint Gate.

For Mike on A day, 1st July 2013.
Class of 2017

Ps & Qs

Little children ought to learn

To say their Ps and Qs.

There's something in a magic word

That parents can't refuse.

And if you're lucky, when they're grown

To teen years and beyond,

The habit sticks and courtesy

Becomes a common bond.

If not, a thoughtless disrespect

Casts shadows that may mar

The reputation of the young,

Who one day may go far!

Loved ones know there's no intent

To denigrate a gift,

But taking things for granted

Seems rude and gets short shrift.

Ps and Qs take little time,

A word in cyberspace

Can make a world of difference,

And love lights up a face.

So if your time is precious,

And preoccupied your mind,

Don't forget those little Ps and Qs-

They'll smooth your way, you'll find.

SPECIES FAECES

All species pass faeces,
This fact is well known.
Only that of the dog
Is received with a moan.
It incurs retribution,
With fines and disdain-
Our four-legged friend
Brings us blushes of shame.

Though, out in the country-
side's rural domain,
You'll find faeces of species
All over the lane.
There are horses for courses
And rabbits and wrens,
There are badgers and foxes,
Cows, gooses and hens.

You must mind where

You're treading,

Yet no one complains.

It's slurped across countryside,

Washed in by rains.

It nurtures the harvest

Which, threshed, milled and sacked,

off to the factory, with sugar it's packed.

Whatever you fancy

to keep you afloat,

Cornflakes or Shreddies

or just porridge oats.

By truck or by train

to the market it goes.

We buy it for breakfast,

And nobody knows?

A POLITICALLY INCORRECT AND DISCRIMINATORY WARNING

Never work for the NHS,
There ain't much pay and you don't progress,
And the years go by and the debts get high.
He's going bald and she's getting fat,
And they all live together in a council flat:
Four kids, three dogs, ten cats.

And don't go teaching in them there schools,
Where nobody learns and the pay's for fools,
And the years go by and the debts get high,
And he goes bald and she gets fat,
And they all live together in a council flat:
Four kids, three dogs, ten cats.

And if a policeman you think you'll be,
The thieves you catch will all go free,
And the years go by and the debts get high,
And the kids grow up and the dogs all die,
And he's gone bald and she's got fat,
And they're evicted from the council flat,
By the council rats!

FEAR

Beloved, I cannot let you go, not yet;
Fate cannot be so cruel to strike a blow so soon,
That I shall not be able to forget the love we shared,
The children of that love not old enough to do without you.
Nor I, who have so recently found out that we are but one being,
So it cannot be that having found that joy,
So soon must fate divide us, dull that glow
Which years of learning, understanding, bought the love
that now I know.

How must it be that, having learned to give and take
Before my slow wits formulate the words to tell you
of my new found learning,
Man must strike you down, with swift intensive savagery that makes
a mockery of this newfound thing, this yearning.
Lord, myself I give, take me that I may have
a few more hours to let him know I love him.
Let me not be too late to be by his side.

7TH DECEMBER 2013

Didn't mean to make you grumpy,
Didn't mean to make a fuss,
Just rang with Birthday Greetings,
'Cos you mean a lot to us.

We have loved you since forever,
You may never know how much,
Though your love for little Arlo
May indicate a touch.

Little boys grow into men,
While Mums and Dads grow old and grey,
And love links the generations,
As we go our different ways.

We never find the right time,
To catch you at your ease,
For you live a busy lifestyle,
And we do our best to please.

We appreciate the support you give
To us, when we are ailing.
We always try to do the same
For you, though often can't help failing.

When old, we live vicariously.
And want to know too much,
It's only that we love you,
And we like to keep in touch.

So in this week of birthdays,
Amid your busy days,
We're always sending love and hugs
To speed you on your way.

HAPPY BIRTHDAY

ARLO'S POEM

Arlo was a beaver, now he is a cub,
Invested on his birthday, he's really in the club.
Take him to a climbing wall and watch him shimmy up,
Surfing, swimming, kayaking, he's quite an active chap.

Give him a box of Lego, watch hand and brain engage.
Everyday is busy, he must be all the rage.
He keeps his Dad and Mummy on their toes with all his doings,
Granddad cannot wait 'til he can sample Granddad's brewing'.

It doesn't seem five minutes he was just a babe in arms,
And soon the years that hurry by will bring teenage alarms.
Before you know it, he will have a family of his own,
And his Dad will be a Granddad and his Mum will be a Nan.

What goes around will come around for that's what life's about,
And everybody gets a chance to learn to work it out.
Life can be a struggle, for some it seems like fun,
It can be quite a puzzle to find what's right for one.

I think and wonder, hope and pray our lad will find his place,
With his Mum and Dad to guide him, he'll run a lively race.
I hope I'm there to see him mature into a man,
But if it's not to be, I will watch from where I am.

There will be love and wonder and a wide world to explore.
I have a feeling he will roam and knock on every door,
And when he finds his place in life and wants to settle down,
With loyalty and courage he will make the world his own.

ABBY

Abby is a dancer, she is also rather brainy.

Abigail is beautiful, she can also be quite zany.

She's a lot of fun to be around, if you can stand the pace.

This soon to be a teenager has a very cheeky face.

She'll cause her Mom some trouble and not a little strife.

I hope we'll see her growing up to take her place in life.

The world can be her oyster, if she keeps on working hard.

She has a sense of humour, she can be quite a card.

She is the only child at home now, Michael has departed.

Enjoying being number one, she's not quite broken hearted!

With just two women in the house, life can get quite exciting,

They need a man to calm things down, especially when they're fighting.

A knight of old, whose heart is bold, to cope with warring women,

A man of some experience, whose hearts with love, are winning.

He'll pour oil on troubled waters, bring back laughter with a tease,

And arms will comfort Carolyn in spite of Abby's pleas.

And when the storm is over and peace again restored,

When life resumes a calmer pace, admit you're never bored,

The young will one day realise life's not a carousel,

And they'll be back for bucks and hugs to see that all is well.

CHRISTMAS

The spirit of Christmas is a little hard to find
When you're out of work, a dropout, all alone or deaf or blind.
It's not easy to remember goodwill, joy, peace of mind.
And remember that he gave his life because he loved mankind.

MARJORIE

Dryad of the kitchen sink

Softly draped in silk and mink,

Lacquered hands and stylish hair

Belie a hectic day of care,

Of children shrieking, stopped up sink

A family crisis, who would think

To see you glide in glossy crowd

That you were just a mother proud,

This evening dressed in rich veneer

Forgot the days frustrating tear.

THANK YOU

Thank you for this evening,
Thank you for this life,
Thank you for supporting me
Through trouble and through strife.

Thanks for understanding
When I'm hard to understand,
Thanks for putting up with me
When I'm mean and underhand.

Know that I still love you,
No matter what I say,
Know that each year loving grows
In a special kind of way.

Know that, with our children
Though I often make a fuss,
I love them as I love you;
They're a special part of us.

THERE

HAVE

BEEN

CERTAIN

MOMENTS

love and life

FOR M & H

When two people come together
for whom love encompasses mutual respect;
The nurturing of each other's growth,
the sharing of each other's burdens,
the acceptance of faults and weaknesses;
Love can turn these into beautiful strengths
undreamed of separately.

In the warmth of lover's kisses, teases, gifts,
tears are but a shower of rain upon seeds,
Obstacles and setbacks, a cloud passing by.
Two who come together thus, can demonstrate
the height human love can reach,
And even, though rarely, the place beyond,
Where Love itself is known.

MOMENTS

There have been certain moments
Which I've longed to share with you,
A shadow from the setting sun,
A skylark in the blue,
A path of shining silver light
Across a stormy sea-
I long to share these things with you
For all eternity.

The love-light in a mother's eyes
Who shares a daughter's pleasure.
The country night, a blazing pyre,
Bring memories I'll treasure.
When autumn branches lit with gold
From setting sun catch fire,
I long to share these things with you,
Beloved sweet desire.

There have been certain moments
When I've needed you so much;
Soft singing from a violin
My poignant heartstrings touch,

A glimpse of you, a gentle smile
Across a crowded street,
And joy springs up inside of me,
Love's wings direct my feet.

Away from you I hurry,
Lest a burden I become,
But then a stillness in the day-
The dawn of morning sun,
A playful pup, when children laugh,
Or eyes brimful with tears-
I long to share these things with you
Throughout the coming years.

Yet quietly I carry on
And try to keep my place,
Try hard to calm my beating heart
When we come face to face,
And hope that I may gently claim
Affection down the years,
When time a wiser counsel brings
And friendship dries my tears.

UNREQUITED LOVE

How many hours I've spent with you,

How many times I've kissed you.

Sighed in such sweet content with you,

Cried when I've sorely missed you.

Told you and told you how much I cared,

Built all my dreams around you,

Tried to forget, you as if I dared

Think about life without you.

Told not a soul; it would never do.

No one will ever know,

Even you!

FOUND

My heart's desire, my spirit's rest.
When you are near, I'm surely blessed,
Though I belong with another love,
I dearly thank the heavens above
That my soul found you.

Object of my contemplation,
Source of all my meditation,
Delight, enchantment, joy, despair,
I suffer love, I only care
That my soul found you.

I sleep, and in my dreams I find
That you are with me, gentle, kind.
A night of wild imaginings,
Of tears and laughter. Morning brings
The thought, I found you.

Safe and secure, contentment grows,
Though you're not mine, yet heaven knows,
To find in life my spirit's rest
I know that I am truly blessed
That my soul found you.

LOVE'S THORN

Yours is the love that keeps my soul alive,
The goal of my endeavour, why I strive,
The thorn within my heart, exquisite pain,
The piercing shaft of sunlight after rain.

Keep my soul alive, guide me as I strive.
Be the balm for that exquisite pain,
That I might, by your grace, Heaven gain.

DOUBT

'I love you', there, it's said, the words are out,
Soft spoken, hesitating, not from doubt.
I doubt not that I love you, only fear
that these are not the words you wish to hear.

I search your face, the loving face oft' dreamed,
For signs of love, but perhaps it only seemed
As if the love in me was swift returned.
Perhaps now it's time I got my fingers burned.

But wait, can I detect a flickering light?
A soft and tender smile, that's of delight?
And shall I feel at last your warm embrace?
And find within your arms my resting place?

HOPE

When I have seen this duty through,
I'll turn at last in trust to you,
And maybe days that seemed so long
Will change to laughter, joy and song.

MORNING

A ship sails round the headland,
A wave laps at the shore,
The crescent moon fades with the light,
Dawn's shadows cross the moor.
A dense and distant clinging mist
Gives up its tenuous hold,
As grey gives way to pink and green
And wispy clouds turn gold.

Impatiently, I wait to see
The sun glide into view,
And, through the gilded fading mist,
I first caught sight of you.
The smile I seem to know so well
Spread slowly 'cross your face
You greeted as a well-known friend,
A stranger to this place.

Soon our paths will separate,
As homeward bound we fare,
But meanwhile, in this silent dawn,
This beauty we can share.

FREEDOM OF SPEECH

It seems that in this workers' age
Free speech has lost its way.
It's got a bit one-sided
As to who can have his say.

Before the unions came along,
The worker was downtrodden,
But now he sings a different song
And life is much more modern.

The leaders shout encouragement
'to stand up for your rights';
'Tis a very small minority
Go hungry through the nights.

Strike, they say, for parity,
Walk out for civil rights,
Back that man for doing his job,
We'll show them how to fight.

The lone voice of an honest man
Who puts his point of view,
Is shouted down and ridiculed-
'To Coventry with you.'

I would that speaking freely
Was for each and every man,
Not just the union-minded
But for every man that can.

Each person has a story,
A different point of view,
It seems that since the unions grew,
It means just them, not you!

DESIRE

Will he accept this foolish whim,
A token of my love for him,
Who hardly knows that I exist
Or want to be by him once kissed?

I cannot tell him how I care,
For he must breathe a different air,
While I mere female one of many,
Can raise a smile, as, two a penny
Hearts around him fall and break,
And from apart, I watch I ache.

An impish fate beleaguers him.
How can he bear the silly grin
Each lovelorn female throws at him?
How can he be so taken in?
Or, gentle natured, does he see
Each cry for tenderness each plea?
Is he aware of love in me?
Oh heaven, have mercy, set me free

I want him. Curse this foolish heart
That aches when we are far apart.
Yet he has chose a different life
That has no need for child or wife,
And if he had, how could it be
That he would e'er consider me?

Yet, if he did, how tenderly
Would I caress him, leave him free
To do his chosen work, his life,
And lovingly I'd be his wife.
And kindly treat each lonely soul,
That needed him to make life whole.

DYING

Free from these aches, these tears, this pain,

Drugged drifting soul recalls the misty rain.

The girl inside me free to roam in dreams of yesterday,

Loose the tightening weights that keep me anchored where I lay.

Free to search and longing for someone to understand,

And tenderly he smiles at me and reaches for my hand.

Then, swift confusion, drifting mist, is this the love I lost?

Oh wretched memory behave, yet still the wires are crossed.

Be still that I may sift and search, recall emotions lost,

The doubt, the laughter, tears, despair and in the end, the cost.

Distorted body, locked in pain, afraid, worn out and frail,

If he looks deep within me, will he see my love, or fail.

Perhaps this day I've met the soul that stands apart like me,

He'll know my mind is free to roam through all eternity.

And will it matter that he's young and I am ninety-three

If one day, when this life is done, he'll stand and wait for me?

ALL MY TOMORROWS

My last thought at night, my first in the morning,

My life's central theme, my delight in loves dawning.

My hope for the future, my yesterdays dream,

All my tomorrows in some unknown theme,

Are full of this love that embraces my heart.

There will be no ending, for if we must part,

My love, like a circle will be back at the start.

CLOUDBIRTH

Where mountains tumble into sea, and
Thin-blooded northerners seek winter sun,
I watch the birthing of clouds.

Water molecules coalesce into visibility,
Teasing the mind with the illusion of life.

Earth turns, a gaseous cauldron rises lazily
From silver sea, morning blue gives birth.

Brief forms mingle with the fingers of God.
Sol climbs warming deserted beaches.

An hour of life expands, contracts and disappears.
Something, then nothing.

HATE

Unhealthy hate is hate suppressed,

While healthy hate is hate expressed.

Resentment is part of the former,

While anger's frustration is warmer,

And when the bubbling pot explodes,

And words leap out like angry toads,

Emotion that's felt and feelings expressed,

In the long run are better than feelings suppressed.

LONGING

Today it has come home to me and strong,
You're part of life to which I can't belong.
Occasionally your presence seems so near,
Unbidden to my eye there springs a tear.
I need you, love.

A sudden sadness crept into my heart.
A wise but unkind fate tore us apart.
Your gentle, oft'- remembered kiss goodbye
Reminded me of you and brought this sigh.
I need you, love.

I see your lovely smile each time I sleep,
Each tear a mirrored image when I weep.
Sweet memories of the few hours we shared,
The joy when I discovered that you cared.
I need you, love.

The understanding when at last I knew
The spirit in my heart was part of you,
And like a wave that breaks upon the shore,
A small part of the greater, evermore.
I love you, love.

FROM WIDGERY CROSS

Below, the sleepy valley silent lies.
I watch the patchwork fields through drowsy eyes,
A distant cuckoo raiding other's nests,
The sunlit sparkling stream pursues its quests.

The close-cropped moorland grass, with sheep like dots
Swift-moving lizards dart among the rocks,
The greys and greens and browns of brackened hills
With peace and joy the tired spirit fills.

Across the summer sky, soft cotton clouds
Are blown into weird shapes like drifting shrouds.
An unseen wind that soft caressed my brow
Brings your distant presence to me now.

A lamb so white we thought it gleamed like snow
Touched with black at ankles, knees and nose,
Its anxious shaggy parent, muddy-faced,
The family urging me to make more haste.

The beauty of this wild, sparse-wooded moor,
And you immersed in distant desert chore.
I will my peace and joy across the hills
And pray that, while I draw this grace within,
'Twill strengthen you with love and inner peace.

MOLLIE

You opened my eyes, you set me free,
You taught my soul to search and see,
You showed me a love that friends could share,
A different love from family care.
You answered my questions and lightly guided,
My inept remarks you gently chided.
Many the moments we shared and chattered,
The world shut out but for friends who mattered.
I only knew you in later years,
But tried my poor best to still some of your fears.
I only know that you are one of the few
Whom I'll love 'til it's my turn to be with you.

THE QUEST

As guiding light and shining star,
Your words of joy brought me this far.
What else delight in store for me-
This quest to find eternity,
Through Him whose love you understand,
I know His is the guiding hand,
But yours, the light that led the way,
That bade my soul submit today.
The more I look, the more I find,
The more I love, the more I mind
The wasted hours and years behind,
But forward now to find the way-
No more concern for yesterday.

SUMMER

The strident cry of seagulls
Breaks the quiet summer day.
The poignant call of curlew
Echoes softly cross the bay.
The misty sun is haloed
In a mackerel-clouded sky
A playful breeze teases the sand,
Tempting it to fly.

The soar and dive of swallows
Finds an echo in my heart.
The moments of togetherness,
Then weeks and months apart,
The loving warmth of nearness,
The sorrow when we part,
The gentle resignation
To a course we couldn't start.

The silent flight of dragonfly,

The drowsy hum of bee,

The silver gleam of water

Is your love alive in me;

Together we shall wander

Through the wonderland of life.

With you as guide and mentor,

I am ever free from strife.

ACORN

A boy had a dream,
An old man struggled between two hills.
Try as he might he was unable to reach the top alone.
The boy vowed to help.

Years passed.

The young man had a dream.
He shared it with a girl, it wasn't her dream.

He turned away, searching.
His quest took him to many hearts.
He learned to love, though not to receive.

Years passed.

He sought the sublime it turned away.
He thought it was he who failed.
Many souls sought the Holy in him
He strived to meet their needs, yet knew not love.

He asked, "How shall I know love?"

One came; she had a dream.
It was not his dream.
She struggled to free the Holy from the human,
Discovered they were one, shared her truth.

She met a need he had not known was there.
They walked between two hills.
In her eyes, he saw the reflection of his soul,
In a flower caught in her hair, he saw the reflection of nature,
In her love, a reflection of the Holy.

She rejoiced in her humanity for, in her, nature was joyful,
In her heart, love, in her soul, the sublime,
Though she knew not these things.

Years passed.

An old man struggled to climb out of a steep valley.
An old woman vowed to help.
His gaze was fixed unwavering on the hill above,
Hers fixed on his back with love.

Wearily, he paused, an old question on his lips,
'What shall I see when I turn at last to see His gaze?'
He glanced back, and saw the answer in her eyes.

SURPRISE

I looked from my window
And what did I see?
A rather wet robin,
Now why should that be?
He was somewhat bedraggled
And rather surprised,
For a warm golden sun
Shone from cloudless blue skies.

He fluffed up his feathers
And spread them to dry,
While keeping a lookout
With one wary eye.
Remembering duty,
He flew to his nest,
Where his neat little lady
Laid four of the best.

They took it in turns
To watch out and to eat,
Each hoping the other
Would not get wet feet.
But day after day,
They awoke to a shower,
Long before breakfast,
Too early an hour.

The moral is clear-
If you know about plumbing,
Don't build your nest
Where a drain pipe is running.

THE WOUNDS OF THE WORLD

He walked an empty shore.
Wind tugged at his upturned collar.
Sea birds shrieked as a wild sea beat at sandstone cliffs.

He had not realized how very tired he was
Until he heard the concern in her voice-
Love knew the cost of caring.

From a distance she seemed shrouded in grey mist.
Sea spray clung to her hair, moistened her face like tears.
She reminded him of the sea, bathing the wounds of the world.

He found himself sharing the burden,
And, in the telling, found it to be lightened.
Meeting her eyes, he forgot himself,
And the light was kindled once more, in his own.

THE BEECH WOOD

By chance, it seems I came across
a cottage in a wood.
Many a day I passed close by,
not knowing where it stood.
Perhaps the home of keepers past,
whose woodland children knew,
Its seasons and its secrets
as year by year they grew.
A thousand years from now will show
an ancient family home,
A lifetime's loves and memories
encroaching trees entomb.
"The woods are lovely, dark and deep,
and I have promises to keep."*
Perhaps, who knows, when these are done,
a home like this, a hallowed one,
In woods as lovely dark and deep
with no more promises to keep,
The Autumn of our lives we'll share,
expressed at last a lifetime's care.

*from Stopping by Woods on a Snowy Evening by Robert Frost

LOVE'S WHISPER

Did I imagine all, was nothing there?
No fingers brushing mine, no warm embrace,
No quiet house, no game to share,
Or wine to dull the pain, no precious face
Lit up with laughter, brimming with a tease?
Did I dream I moved to turn away
In sudden shyness, and gentle hands held me tenderly?

Did I imagine, one November eve,
With flickering glow of apple-scented logs
And fireside drowsiness and silences,
Was there no symphony, no talk of love,
Or of impossibilities, or hope?
And did I dream I turned to leave reluctantly
And was held close and kissed; was love affirmed?

Did I imagine all, was there no pain,
No soft encouragement in that embrace,
No need fulfilled or sorrow shared?
Was there no comforting when once I phoned,
When tiredness filled your voice, sadness your heart,
For human need had touched your very soul?
Did you not reach for me across an aching void?

Love whispers, "All was so".

SUBSTITUTION

I have closed my eyes and seen your face before me.
I have dreamed of butterflies and stirred, still dreaming,
To feel your eyelashes brushing my cheek.
I have awakened to moonlight streaming in at my window
And seen your head on my pillow.
I have listened to your stillness in the depth of night.

I have watched buds open, birds sing, in the warm sun of a spring day
And felt tiredness descend upon me and known it was yours.
I have known that you have thought of me,
And, in that moment, passed over the burden of your weariness,
Sure that it is willingly taken, that you may carry on.
I open mind and heart to that burden joyfully,
And offer love to Love.

THE QUESTION

'How can I experience love except by a lover's proofs,
Whispers, kisses, letters, gifts and shining eyes?'
'How shall I know love, how shall I know it's real?
How can I experience it? I don't know what to feel.'

THE ANSWER

'Listen for the whisper that floats upon the breeze.
Look for shy and shining eyes, low laughter, gentle tease,'
Tread softly lest it fly away and, like a butterfly, 'twill stay.'

TOGETHER

One day, when this life is done,
In God's own Heaven, we shall be one.
I shall be then a part of thee,
And thou shall be a part of me.

THE VISIT

Today's events have passed as in a dream.
Like fading memories, they almost seem
As if they never happened, yet, sweet love,
For a few hours you and I were close,
Drawn each together in the common bond.

A thoughtless uttered word, a swift retort,
And both of us too late to cool the heat
of swiftly rising temper. She the one
bewildered, he defiant, in defeat,
and you, the pawn, the subject of the feud

An unimportant incident, a slight
But jarring note in such a perfect day,
And yet, I wondered, did to each occur
The thought that, though they differed, yours the hurt,
The dear forgiving soul that feels the pain.

Perhaps sweet love imagines each small slight,
The loving heart defending the beloved.
Yet, dearest, sure I am and right
That each harsh word touches your whole being
And leaves another mark upon the soul.

THE LETTER

Beloved, who knows me better than any other,
Who accepted my love yet couldn't say, 'I love you',
Who never answered letters, yet treasured my endless calls,
Who 'basked in my love', your words not mine.
How painful were the times of yesteryear!
Being in love mellowed into loving.
We laughed and teased in the armchair comfort of
Unconditional love, neither asking nor giving,
Just Being.

Then you went away. I wept, I mourned,
And then discovered love lasts forever,
Love does not die.
Came a time, our love reached out to others,
Made me strong.

Snatched hours and hallowed days;
Our walks in the woods,
Evenings by flickering flames,
Bruch's concerto,
Too much wine,
A shared embrace.

You are always there in ways words cannot show.
You are in me and I in you.
We visit still the depth of tranquil wood,
We stand before the crashing of the waves,
The places that you loved, still ours,
For you are always with me.
When I die, yours is the face,
The love, that brings me home.

EVENING

Slowly the sun dips to its evening rest,
Its mellow light calling each bird to nest,
The winged spirits on their joyful quest
Submit to greater Love that knows them best.

One unbound spirit soars on tireless wings,
High in the paling sky, joyful it sings,
Across the shadowed valley, its song rings,
As to each trembling heart, the skylark sings.

Silenced at last, it drifts into the night
Humbled by beauty, gold and crimson light,
In glorious mantle, Earth meets Love tonight,
Showing her joy with blushes of delight.

The trees upon the hill are touched by fire;
Two lovers in the valley, with desire
Cling to each other, while a distant choir
Sings, like the lark, a chorus to Messiah.

TONIGHT

I am tired tonight and I miss you

And long for you, love, through tears,

And somehow the days and weeks and months,

Are beginning to feel like years.

I am thinking tonight of the passion

That you kindled in my heart

And wonder if time will cool the flames

Of desire, now that we're apart.

OF LOVE AND LIFE

If music be the food of love,
Then verse must be its wine,
For poetry is to the heart
As wisdom to the mind.

Then am I wise to lose my heart
To sing your praise this way?
Yet every full moon has its night,
And every fool his day.

FRIENDS

Remember the moments that I longed to share with you-
A skylark in the setting sun, the feel of morning dew,
The view across the valley from a high and windy hill,
A gentle kiss, a poem shared my wildest dreams fulfilled.

The moments when I needed you when somehow you were there,
The times of sweet uncertainty until I knew you cared.
How well I know that certain smile that calms my aching heart,
How much I love the gentleness that is my missing part.

Time brought that wiser counsel that enabled me to see
That each cameo of nature brings your love alive for me.
If whatever's in the future brings us joy or brings us tears,
I know the passion and the passiveness of love will last the years.

SYCHBANT - UCHAF

Here in this ruined cottage in the wood
Might some great-grandchild see the broken hearth,
Still stained with smoke that fifty years of rain
Have not washed clean. Two rafters, green with moss,
Crumble between the fallen blocks of stone
That later roots have lifted and thrown down.
Encroaching trees scarce let the ruins breathe.
All will go under, yet beneath the earth
A thousand years from now, one still could show
The fixed foundations of this family home,
Dig up memorials to love and life.
We'd envy such a child her certain proofs.
Our lives are lived in homes of other men,
Our love, proscribed, can neither build nor breed.
So since we cannot hallow one such place,
Let all like places everywhere be ours.

STOLEN HOURS

How I have loved my stolen hours with you,

Discovering each other as friends do.

THE HAND OF TIME

I cling to things that give me pleasure-

Your smile, your poetry and mine.

Some let these go, they've had their measure

Not I, they mellow as good wine

laid down to wait the hand of time.

WINTER

Robin Redbreast strutting smartly
Through the crisp and icy snow
You must have polished bright your feathers
Have you very far to go?

Perhaps you have to see a lady
Is that why your red breast glows?
Or perhaps it's just to brighten gladly
Cheer our hearts through winter snows.

SNIPPETS

Today is yesterday tomorrow
And tomorrow's yesterday.
What then is tomorrow?

Love a little,
Laugh a little,
Extend a helping hand.
A smile will light another's world
And leave them feeling grand.

I smiled and the stranger was you.

THE SEEKER

a spiritual journey

THE SEEKER

The days when my soul goes wandering
To find the eternal thread,
Leaves hearth and home like an empty shell-
These are the days I dread.
When nothing is me, when husband and
Children with clouded eyes
Look to the centre and find it bleak,
Like the moor under threatening skies.

I know where my soul goes wandering,
Where the sky and the hilltops meet,
Where deer softly graze
In the damp morning haze,
Where creatures are born
And the winter's forlorn
And I'm lost in the mist.

In the deepest shade of the darkest wood,
Where the searching soul meets its self,
Where the spirit of earth is the spirit of man,
Where light in the trees plays "catch if you can",
I am.

LIFE

Life is like a country lane,

It twists and turns and starts again.

In wooded parts, it hems you in,

Then opens to a country scene.

In summer sun and winter snows,

It travels on. Where? No one knows.

The sunlit patches are joys of life,

The shady parts, the pain and strife.

It twists and turns and forks and then

It doubles back and starts again.

Here a brook and there a nest,

A sheltered bank that offers rest,

A brief respite along the way,

A time for toil, a time for play,

A chance to look at yesterday,

And, if you choose, a time to pray.

THE CEDAR

Stark against a winter sky
A mighty cedar. Clouds pass by,
A gentle breeze your branches bend,
And gracefulness to beauty lend.

THE CHRISTMAS BABE

The empty cot stands waiting.
Expectant mothers rest.
Along the quiet corridors
The nurses sing with zest.
'The holly and the ivy'
Floats softly down the ward,
And three wise men at stable door
Pay tribute to their Lord.

The tinselled tree reflects each light,
The Virgin Mother mild
Smiles knowingly around the ward,
While watching her sweet child;
Outside the fathers come and go,
And wait with anxious eye.
Above the crisp and glistening snow
The diamond studded sky.

Those mothers who have given birth
Contented feed their mites,
And others watch and wait and hope,

As nurses dim the lights.
The empty cot is decked with joy
To await the Christmas birth,
Will this year bring a girl or boy
To spread His love on Earth?

Along the empty midnight street
An ambulance comes wailing,
Indoors the midwife hopeful waits,
And hopes this one's not ailing.
The mother, tense and pale with strain,
Her burden will deliver,
Kind hands help, safely ease the pain,
As bells chime 'cross the river.

'It's Christmas morn, they loudly ring,
And across the land, the people sing
Their carols praise the newborn king
Who peace on earth, goodwill will bring;
And as the bells ring out with joy,
The mother holds her baby boy,
A message whispered through the night,
'The Christmas baby's born 'All's right!'

A CAROL
(Tune: Lord of the dance)

I wander through the country lanes and see the berries red,
And in my mind, I see a crown of thorns upon his head.
Then I see the mistletoe, hanging on the bough,
And remember and rejoice: the king of kings born now.

Chorus
Joy, joy a child is born today.
He comes to bring salvation, if we listen and we pray.
He comes to show us goodness and he comes to bring us love.
He comes to us in Glory from the Lord above.

The Virgin watches tenderly that first and feeble yawn.
Contentment grows inside of her; the Holy child is born.
He's come, fulfilled the prophecy to wise men and the rest.
She brushes 'side the sorrow that lies heavy in her breast.

Chorus

The wise men and the shepherds come to show him their respect.
The donkeys and the cattle warm around him they collect.
To cherish and to nurture close this babe from up above,
Sent to us as Saviour by our God of Love.

Chorus

MORNING

The silent morn awakens,
His glory fills the sky.
I slip from bed and rub the dust
Of sleep from round my eyes.

Some strange insistent calling
Draws me high up to the hill.
Though thin the clothes that cling to me,
With glorious joy I fill.

With hope and love, I worship
My God, who made this land,
Who made us all and watches us
And guides with gentle hand.

Somehow I know he watches
The chaos that we make.
It's not for me to understand
Why man won't give, just take.

His the infinite wisdom that
Dreamed the eternal plan.
His the hand that steers the course.
And makes the God of man.

A HYMN
(Tune: Greensleeves)

The Christ has come to light the way.
He walks beside us through each long day,
And when we're lost He shows the way.
He died to become our Saviour.

Chorus

His love is my desire ,
His goodness shines in our darkest hour.
He came on a winter's morn,
And He died to become our Saviour.

He comes with comfort, he comes with joy,
He comes for children, each girl and boy.
He comes for rich and He comes for poor,
And He died to become our Saviour.

Chorus

I know not why, but He cares for me.
He shows the way we can all be free.
He'll light the path to eternity,
And he died to become our Saviour.

Chorus

We pray for wisdom, we pray for truth,
Believe in faith, do not ask for proof.
Invite Him in, do not stand aloof,
He died to become our Saviour.

Chorus

His love is my desire,
His goodness shines in our darkest hour.
He came on a winter's morn,
And he died to become our Saviour.

'TIL WE HAVE FACES

'Til we have faces, I must blunder on
in search of truth, such truth as I can find.
Am I a part of that of which I seek?
So many questions crowding through my mind.

Foolhardy, centred inwards on myself,
Searching outwardly for inward truth
In seeking such, of what? I know not what,
How can I know it if indeed it's there!

It's there! That much I know, else why this need,
This deep yet empty longing in my soul?
On other's wisdom, soul and mind must feed
Until I learn to recognise my goal.

At first, it was a solitary road,
Here straight and narrow, there a twisted mess.
Now so many turnings, which the way?
The tortured soul asks of the heart, confess.

How can the heart confess? It too is lost
Among the cares and trials of this life,
Its temporary solace sought in vain.
Without a guiding light, there's only strife.

And then a spark of light, a word of truth,
Stripped thoughts of worldly riches from my mind,
An unkempt vagrant people walked around,
Hammered at my guilt, bade me be kind.

There in the depths, a light was born,
A spark kindled by love and born of joy,
A strange insistent tugging at my soul,
Directing to Himself my life's employ.

THE RICH MAN'S DAUGHTER

'I want God for Christmas,' the rich man's daughter cried,
'I want God for Christmas.' She would not be denied.
'You want God for Christmas?' the saint beside her smiled.
'If you want God for Christmas, be humble, gentle, child.'

'Humble,' cried the daughter. 'I know not what you mean.'
'Humility and wisdom learn, and joy and love between,
If you want God for Christmas, His servant you must be,
And love him beyond question with sweet humility.'

It's hard for a rich man's daughter to come face to face with God,
But with the Saint to guide her, she followed where he trod.
She walked among the lepers, she supped among the poor,
She followed where the good man led and slept on unswept floor.

She came as ministering angel; the poor they called her saint.
She nursed the sick and led the lame 'til she was weak and faint.
When in her sick bed lying, 'My Saviour come,' she prayed.
The saint he watched her dying, he watched and was afraid.

For humility and glory were written in her face-
At last the rich man's daughter found, in God, her resting place.

MYSTERY

Born out of winter, I have come at last to spring,
With wondering eyes new opened, I have found eternal things,
Moments of mystery, not yet understood.
I watch and wait as infant on the verge of childhood;
Yet perhaps, more like a seed of time, or bulb of daffodil,
'Til now a thing deep hidden, in the valley or the hill.
The dawn of spring encourages a slender stem to birth,
A swelling bud, that bursts into its summertime on earth.

The warmth of sun, the wet of rain, the nip of morning frost,
And then the gradual opening of flower, wind gently tossed.
Alone on some quiet window sill, just looking at the world,
Or part of some great myriad host in distant wood unfurled;
Aware for a brief lifetime of beauty all around,
Then dying into mystery, deep down into the ground,
Not ended or begun, the cycle merely carries on,
And I, just like the daffodil, am back where I belong.

IF

If you have no dream, how can you live?
If you have no love, how can you give?
If you have no joy, how can you sorrow?
If there is no today, what of tomorrow?

Take my dream and live,
Take my love and give,
Take my joy and sorrow,
Love today and live tomorrow.

THE CHURCH

Expectantly, with hope and love,
She waits with doors thrown wide,
The chancel steps are decked with flowers
To greet this morning's bride.

White lilies for a virgin,
Sweet daisies, love and joy,
And greenery and fern abound-
She may be shy and coy.

And as she leaves the altar,
And walks back down the aisle,
A special touch, the verger's gift
Where she may pause a while.

Sweet roses framed in veils of white,
Pale pink for friendship new,
A deeper pink, and deeper still,
As their love bloomed and grew.

The last rose, red of deepest hue,
Soft velvet touched with dew,
As, hand in hand, they leave the church
To start their lives anew.

WHAT IS GOD?

What is God?

The inner light, that sees me safely through the night.

Who is God?

The quiet voice that guides me gently, keeps me right.

Where is God?

He is around me like a cloak against the wind.

Why is God?

He is to show me what I am and how I've sinned.

'I am God'

'Within, without and all about you. Love me.'

ICTHOS

I am

The Christ,

Come to save,

The sign of faith.

Humble fish,

Once Holy

Symbol

Of

Love.

EASTER

Insistent bells were ringing to disturb the veils of sleep,

A golden-haloed sleepy head around the door did peep.

A shaft of silver sunlight told of a glorious dawn,

And slowly I awaken to another Easter morn.

A drive through primrose-scented lanes,

Reflected light on distant panes,

A breeze that lightly ruffles trees,

A silver haze on distant seas.

The child and I walked into church,

Sun mingled flowers fill every perch,

Dust motes dance in beams of light,

All is unveiled from Lent's long night.

A deep and hidden joy that felt

A kinship with each one that knelt.

Awareness grows of spiritual wings,

Thrown off the weight of worldly things.

'Christ is risen,' the parson prays.

'Risen indeed!' The songs of praise

Ring out upon this Easter morn,

As all rejoice, the Christ reborn.

MOVING ON

To show our love in poetry
The incantation read.
Who could resist our vicar's plea?
Not this poetic maid.
So here, dear priest, with twinkling eye,
Accept our adoration.
We love you more as years go by,
Saint Andrew's congregation!

THE GIFT

You have the gift that's given
Only to a chosen few-
The gift of loving glorious joy,
That's shared in caring too.
And when those doubts assail you,
That come to each loving soul,
Remember you belong to Him-
His love will make you whole.

FAREWELL

Farewell, dear priest with twinkling eye,
How years have swiftly tumbled by.
For each of those you leave behind,
There's doubts, uncertainties in mind.
One wonders perhaps 'How shall I cope,
Has God withdrawn my only hope?'
Another ill conceals his tears,
Recalls kind words of yesteryears.
Yet others smile and turn away,
Pre-occupied by yesterday.

While you are here, some mock or moan
That from our midst your care has flown.
And, as the weeks and months pass by,
Shall we recall each tear, each sigh,
Or fickle, frail as folks are made,
As time slips by and memories fade,
Shall gentle friendship forged with love
Be swift forgot; or from above
Will He remind us with His care,
His is our priest whom we must share?

The wind of change blows constantly,
Else perhaps we'd all complacent be.
Each soul must learn to stand alone,
To face the world out on his own.
Each test of faith seems hard to bear,
As if the light of Love's aware.
That we must draw on spiritual strength,
Our priest has sermoned us at length,
That God with love plays hide and seek,
Forsakes the proud and saves the weak.

Though you move on and we remain,
We know you've shared our joy our pain;
Each one would give, if each could speak,
His thanks for you, when faith was weak.
God keep you, Father in His care-
Our love goes with you and our prayers.
Maybe, in sharing, we can find
Some inner joy who stay behind,
Drawn close in friendly harmony,
Discovering Him who guided thee.

SUMMER RETREAT

Peace, which passes understanding,
Found me 'neath these quiet trees,
Winged spirits closely venture-
Birds and butterflies and bees.

Softly glittering like diamonds,
Morning dew makes emerald grass.
Sheltered in the arms of heaven,
For earthbound spirits peace at last.

Cedar rests in gentle splendour;
How it moans in summer storm,
Oaks, majestic, watch protecting,
Clad in summer's gayest form.

Paths through gardens, wild and wending,
Swing that offers sweet repose,
Water gardens, joy unending,
Souls, past and present, wander those.

Place of peace, in death enduring,
Those who sought this solace find
Here the threshold, spirits enter,
Pain and sorrow left behind.

Into his celestial splendour,
Arms of love flung open wide,
All the throng of Heaven rejoicing,
Saints and angels at his side.

We, who to the world returning,
Granted gifts of joy and peace,
Captured in a day of stillness,
In this quiet and lovely place;

Outward must reflect his glory,
In faith and love and humble pride.
We, the lambs, must spread the story
Of the shepherd crucified.

SUMMER RAIN

I watch the distant fields through sodden trees.
A somber sky hangs heavy over these,
Even the swallows, silent in the eaves,
Wait patiently for summer's morning breeze.

Watching the world through jewel-encrusted pane,
Diamonds of dew, the sun can make of rain.
The steady tick of clock would make one feign
Remember this observer's silent pain.

All those around me, deep in thought or book,
Each seeking her own way, one smiling look
Encourages me. I find that I am not alone,
But corporate one searching the true way home.

FISH

I am Fish
Translated, I am Icthos in the Greek.

Humble Fish,
Once holy symbol when of Christ none speak.

A Sign,
When men of faith were murdered for believing.

Of Christ,
That they may gather close, His love receiving.

The Fish,
A worthy meat for Christ, the Holy One.

The Food,
That He partook when resurrection had begun.

The Sign,
When Jonah was flung back upon the shore.

Of Love,
That He cares for each one, for evermore.

THE YOUNG ONES

They came to the wise man and lingered a while
One plucked up courage and asked with a smile

Who is to die, who is to live?
Who is to take, who is to give?
Who is to wonder, who is to know?
Who is to show us the path we must go?
Who is to plant, who is to sow?
Who is to reap the crops that I grow?

Who rules the sea, makes it calm makes it storm?
Who builds my house, keeps me sheltered and warm?
Who gives me knowledge, puts skill in my hands?
Who sends the rain that keeps fertile my lands?

He paused,

But the wise man kept silent and smiled,

A smile that kept watchers entranced and beguiled.

Around them grew silence; a sweet heady scent

Perfumed the air, which hung heavy and lent

An air of detachment; with wonder and awe,

They watched as a glow filled the sky and the sea,

And a voice in each mind whispered silent and free,

I am Creator.

Creation, Love Me.

GENII LOCI
(Spirit of Place)

No battlemented tower stands guard above this church,

No soaring spire of ancient heritage can save this place from

Budget-minded bishops.

Not for us a Grade One listed reprieve. A church is its people,

the erudite proclaim, mesmerised by falling rolls,

a church is its people.

Ay! People make the church and spirits of people past.

Here, rites of passage mark the way of time,

Those who worked the sea and farmed the land, passed on.

You who enter here to sit and rest, and seekers of peace,

you are all here eternally.

Here too, the blessed priests of yesteryear.

Their spirits linger, melding with the flock, adding to

the Spirit of this place; it touches all who enter.

St Andrew waits, his net thrown wide, to offer peace that life's denied,
A sacristan, both old and grey, has watched the generations pray,
Each found a quiet favoured place, to ask forgiveness, pray for grace,
St Nicholas stands gaunt, severe, recalling those who worshipped here.

Above him, stark against red bricks, carved agony the crucifix.
Yet, from her place, the Blessed Maid looks down serene and unafraid,
From leaded windows, multi-stained, the peoples of the Bible framed,
Before the Blessed Sacrament (in ancient times with garment rent),
Past priests, in anguish and despair, have knelt in penitential prayer.

These times will swift seem memory, though not in Christ's eternity,
Future, past, all time is now, contained within itself somehow.
It's not for us to reason why, accept a hidden truth, we try
to understand, beyond the grave, His promise that all will be saved.

Though we must lose this much-loved place, it lives eternally in grace.
Nothing that ever is, is not. When time stands still, this Holy Plot
Will still be here for you to find, like some hid secret in the mind.
The spirit rests, yet lives eternal, while we endeavour the diurnal.

THE WORD

In the beginning was the WORD,
And the word was ONE.
And ONE was LOVE

Love spread throughout all that is. Love was exploring, expanding, finding new frontiers of being, finding inner space.
At last, Love the One, the Word, was still; and, in the stillness, contemplated its being. In its contemplation, it reflected upon its oneness, its vastness, its infinity.

Love was unseeable, unknowable, immeasurable, being all, containing all within itself. It could be turbulent, wild, uncontrolled. Yet Love could be still.

From the centre of its stillness, Love contemplated its own dimensions, its vast infinities, still, calm.

Love became aware of its unity; this awareness was Consciousness. Consciousness contemplated, explored its oneness. In its contemplation, Love discovered a need it hadn't known was there. It discovered a yearning in its oneness. It discovered a need for companionship. As it wanted companionship, the stillness began to glow. The glow grew in vast rippling waves, expanding out from its centre.

Conscious, it stopped, the glow stopped. It contemplated the glow and called this LIGHT. Beyond the glow was NOT LIGHT. It noted the difference. It looked upon the light and was comforted; it went on creating. Came a time when stars and planets, suns and moons were created. On one planet, with one moon, time came. There followed mountains and seas. In the seas, creatures formed. One day a creature climbed upon the land. At last came man, and the Creator was no longer alone.

NIGHT VISION

Before the stars were born, eternal night.
Before that great event, the birth of light,
YOU ARE.

Some call you 'No Thing' 'Emptiness'
Others, 'All that is' 'The Ultimate'.
You named yourself, 'I am'.

Awareness grew and watched the void fill up.
Space-time was born.
You called the darkness night, and daylight, morn.

And all that fled Event Horizon's birth
Grew to become the stars, the planets, earth.
Countless galaxies gave birth to time
As gases cooled, condensed and turned to slime.

Energies' purest form, YOU,
Of all, in all, observer and observed.
Expansive consciousness, filled, loved,
all the void that was before;

And knew its solitude beyond infinity.
Played with the gaseous winds and danced with light.
Awareness sent the startled stars to adorn the night.

'No Thing', yet 'all in all',
designed the pairs we know,
and peopled earth in your own image formed,
and made us what we are.

The cosmos mirrored in the smallest cell,
There, too, you lodge,
The presence in the space within,
as also in the solar wind.

You gave us choice: discover what we are,
Or disregard, forget
the birth of being we were witness to.
We, too, are part of you.

This then is my creed, I grew up believing in ' In the beginning was the word and the word was love'. Later education gave me a scientific understanding of the ' Big Bang' theory, I used to think they were mutually exclusive, now I believe they are but aspects of the same phenomenon.

THE RELUCTANT CHRISTIAN

Ancient stories point a way
I should or should not go,
And ancient stories demonstrate
The way that leads to woe.

I've listened to the doctrine,
Questioned sin and creed and worth,
Heard the birthing and diminishment
Of those ancient feet on earth.

Heard fundamental doctrine preached,
Interpreted by others.
Have walked away, rejecting
Words that left me smothered.

What is this deep-felt, hidden thing
That tells me I believe,
That reaches out and finds itself?
I look, but can't perceive.

Through darkness, fears and searching,
The ancient myths persist.
They have a power to touch me,
Where other men resist.

From deep within a silence,
In the stillness of the day,
The hint of something tangible—
Somehow I know the way.

A deep thing, like the mystery
Given birth so long ago,
Has the power to speak to me,
And grace to make it so.

CREDO

I believe in the Mystery at the centre of all that is. That this Ultimate Mystery is the ground in which my being is rooted, the source that life emerges from at every moment.

It is closer than breathing, thinking, closer than consciousness itself.

Its presence may be felt as we surrender to the attraction of interior silence, tranquillity and peace, letting all else fade.

I believe the Ultimate Mystery to be the godhead to which all world religions can lead us to.

My own way through my Christian faith as valid as that of Islam, Judaism, Buddhism and the many other spiritual pathways.

I believe that the Ultimate Mystery, that which I call God, Love, Wisdom, is in the world and the world is in God.

I believe that this may be the final reality, that we are in God and God is in us, and that all dualities are transcended.

In the silence of contemplative prayer, we surrender to Stillness, to Love, to that Mystery.

In a presence so immense yet so humble, awe-inspiring yet gentle, limitless yet so intimate, tender and personal, that I know that I am known.

Be still and know that I am God.

(*Belief = 1 part faith and 9 parts trust*)

THREE IN ONE

Three is what we were, the poet muses.
Three separate churches, with three different uses,

Three different paths to grace: low, middle, high,
Each shows a different face, each wonders why.

The poet meditates upon the three in one.
Diversity in unity is what we could become.

Father: the mother church high on her hill,
Uniting all within the town, with grace the faithful fill.

Son: the daughter church, her doors in silence closed,
Her faithful moving up the hill, their very souls transposed.

The Holy Ghost, St. Andrews is, wherein our hearts do dwell,
Yet, by his very essence, He is in our souls as well.

It is the Holy Spirit of the father, in the son,
Who gives the deepest meaning to the Holy Three in One.

He who has lived and loved and lost has known the deepest pain,
Whose sorrow carved the deepest wound, these can know love again.

This we three congregations share, all that's familiar lost,
Or so we say, with little faith, who only count the cost.

What can we bring, what can we share, to comfort our tomorrows?
If nothing else, bring him our pain, our human joys and sorrows.

The little church brings children, love and laughter, just in time,
Far reaching faith and fellowship, both simple and sublime.

Can we perhaps bring something too? Diversity in caring,
Mysterium et tremendum, and a gentle way of sharing.

Can you accept our gifts? Can we united be?
In seeking greater truth and love in Holy Trinity.

POSBURY

Lambs to the slaughter,

Lambs to the feast,

Fed by the sisters,

Taught by the priest.

This then, of heaven

Is earth's best endeavour

Sisters of Francis,

Your gifts are forever.

SHELL COTTAGE

It was an awareness, a fleeting impression,
I didn't **see** anything.
We scrambled up rough paths, hewn from the steep valley sides,
Up to a clearing among the bracken known as 'the Hermitage'.
Great granite boulders protected it from view,
unless you knew where to look.
In the tiny cove below, a few Cornish cottages slept,
Waves crashed on rocks that protected the slipway,
And the five small boats pulled high;
Two already out, mackerel running.
Visible below us, the roof and terrace of our retreat.

Five friends, five days, walking, praying, laughing, playing,
Eating, oh yes, eating, like kings in the Aga warm kitchen.
We celebrated daily, on the cliff top at sunrise,
as in some pagan ritual;
In the common room, that was chapel and bedroom to our priest,
old and grey as we,
Even in the kitchen, around the scrubbed deal table.
That was the first morning when, chattering like starlings,
We shared our breaking fast, planning our day's adventures.
Prayers first, of course. Our study time this year?
The Four Quartets.

And then our walks, Porthcurno, Porthgwarra,
the sunken Holy Well below St. Levans Church,
Bathing our aching parts, if we could just bend down that far!
Always hopeful and so blessed; then the scramble down to the beach,
off with shoes and socks, and a paddle in the azure sea.
Then home for lunch!
Climbing Carn Brea to gaze down on Lands End.
Patchwork fields and cliffs, soft-eyed Guernseys that provide
breakfast milk, untouched by Pasteur's hand;
and fresh laid eggs.

Our seventh year in Paradise,
Our last, our retreat to become a family home;
this final morning, the scramble up to the Hermitage at dawn.
Who hadn't we prayed for, even the struggling farmer; and the fishermen,
Those who rose before sunrise, eyed the skies, the wind, the sea,
Before venturing on God's great Atlantic.
One man, an open boat against the changing elements,
Some didn't return!
Even now the clatter of the winch, as another casts off seawards
Our prayers and our eyes follow him, then focus to our task.

Now the fleeting moment, barely an awareness;
Behind our celebrant an impression of… Holiness? Ten-twelve feet
Of something over our bowed heads,
'Heaven and earth are full of thy glory.'
Crowds gather around us and up the valley sides,
a mass of souls, partaking of the Mass,
the world communion there… then gone.
I open my eyes to look, just we few, sharing the bread and wine.
I reach for the hands beside me. Smiling our love,
We stand long seconds, encircling the moment-
a fleeting impression, a presence, there and gone.
Yet something remains.

A PERSONAL LORDS PRAYER

Our Father, in whom I am in heaven,

Hallowed art Thou.

Give me this day to be a channel of thy grace,

That those I have hurt may be healed of their suffering,

as I am healed.

Give all the knowledge of thy eternal Kingdom

Where, now and forever,

We are one in thee.

THE CONGREGATION

Quick to criticise, should we
Loving and forgiving be?
'She drives me mad with all her fuss,'
'The vicar's such an awkward cuss,'
'And you should see the PCC!'
'I don't know why no one asked me,'
'Have you seen the altar flowers?'
'My dear, it must have taken hours,'
'And did you see the produce stall?'
'They call that produce?' after all
'Does anybody have the time?'
Quick to criticise, should we
Loving and forgiving be?

A TIME

A time to love, a time to play,
A time to put the memories away.

A time to sow, a time to reap,
A time to rest and then a time to sleep.

A time to laugh, a time to mope,
A time for darkness and then a time for hope.

A time to live, a time to die,
A time to weep and then a time to sigh.

A time for birth, a time for death,
A time for grace and then a time for faith.

THE GIFT OF LOVE

This is the gift of love,

This peace that comes,

And this; the gift of joy,

This rich outpouring.

Gentle benevolence that bends

Earthward, his inner eye,

And grace embraces

He whom the light enlightens.

THE ANGEL OF DEATH

nearing the end

STRANGE QUIET DAY

Strange, quiet day,

Holding its breath.

Who will come calling?

The angel of death?

Walk into sunlight

On silvery sea.

Whose voice is calling?

Speak softly to me.

Strange silvered shadows

On fast flying clouds,

Shrill seabirds crying

The sea mist enshrouds,

A smile that is gentle,

A voice full of love.

Soft wings transport me

To heaven above.

THE ANGEL

Strange quiet day, holding its breath.
Who will come calling-the angel of death?
A voice full of kindness, a love that is free,
Speak softly stranger, that is calling to me.

Strange quiet eve at the end of the day,
A breath held in waiting, a moment to pray.
We wait for the call from the master above,
Who gathers his children with a heart full of love.

It's hard to be patient, to wait to the end,
To endure each small kindness of nurse or of friend.
Impatient the soul to return to its source-
That timeless, eternal, unknowable force.

RETIRED

The measure of your days now changes;
Days to laze, time for you to pause.
Now time can be sublime.
Your measure for pleasure
Is yours to chose,
The hoped for future now, the past achieved,
The present, now the only true measure of your days.
Enjoy.

ODE TO RETIREMENT

then

All work is done; the years of time are run.
Back in the mists of time, when I was young,
The framework of an eight-hour day begun,
Long days and weary nights, when tiredness clung,
When endless patients entered through swing doors.
Some came and went with quiet cheerfulness,
Others struggled with painful laboured breath.
Where dust was never seen on polished floors,
Where all the care and skills that we possess
Some healed, some held at bay a painful death.

now

Now time has bought release from caring toil.
Time to reflect, adjust to slower pace,
To meditate, take up the poet's foil?
Become an onlooker to life's brief race.
To watch one's children's children grow and play,
And traverse childhood, 'til they come of age
To learn and love, and choose a working life.
And so, once more, the cycle of each day
Turns to the earning of a living wage;
maybe the wielding of a surgeon's knife?

to come

Yet more years pass, and I am old and frail,
Though looking back and lively still in mind.
My children old and theirs now in full sail.
Life's longing for itself complete, defined.
How strange that all the pain, the toil, the love,
We think is ours, what is it we control?
A few decisions here; another may
Be watching over all from high above,
To whom we will return this borrowed soul
When LIFE and LOVE fuse in eternal day.

DEATH RIDES THE NIGHT TRAIN

a lullaby

Death rides the night train.
Hush baby, do not cry.
Death rides the night train.
The devil's flying by,
And if he hears you crying,
The train may stop its rush.
It's seeking souls the whole night through,
So hush, my darling, hush.

Your Daddy drives the night train,
The angels paint the sky.
Your Daddy drives the night train-
Tonight he's going to die,
And if he hears you crying,
He may not stop its rush,
And we must wait the whole night through,
So hush, my darling, hush.

We had to come before him.
Hush baby, do not cry.
St Peter's going to fetch him
Tonight, you'll see, he'll die.
And if he hears you crying,
The train may stop its rush.
The devil must be thwarted,
So hush, my baby, hush.

We've waited here forever.
Hush baby, do not cry.
Tonight you'll see your Daddy-
Tonight he's going to die.
And if he hears you crying,
The devil he will know,
And we must wait the whole night through,
To claim your Daddy's soul.

July 1978 Taunton train fire

YOUTH

I have lived through desolation,
I have sought eternal truth,
I have wrestled with temptation
Since self-centred, thoughtless youth;
Then I flaunted hell's damnation,
And I risked eternal wrath.
Even watched a dying nation,
With an empty callow laugh.

Now the time is for reflection,
Now I have to face the truth.
When I gave in to temptation,
In that empty fruitless youth;
Never thought I'd face the music,
Feel the deep pangs of remorse,
Never understood the meaning,
But I had to run the course.

WAR BIRTH

Poor wee scrap, I drag you from your mother's womb
Into this sorry world that shall become your tomb,
That you could be the one with wisdom filled,
And not another innocent to be killed.
Surely, can heaven and common sense prevail?
Another miracle be born, to find the trail
To freedom.

LAMENT

Child of my child, beloved by me,
If only my son were here to see.
The secret shared, a mother proud,
The golden sun, a feathered cloud.

Hand in hand in hand, your wife and child
Share life and memories of you.
But do not fret, my dearest son
Our life on earth will soon be done,
And we, with you, will wander free.

MY PATIENT

I watch you quietly lying there,
One fair-haired child that needs my care.
Your mother sits beside you deep in prayer,
And tries hard not to let you see despair.

I know, that deep inside, her heart is crying,
For I have had to tell her that you're dying.
Sweet innocent, a part of some great plan,
When you meet Love, please intercede for Man.

THE STAIRWAY OF SURPRISE

A child sleeps,
And, round her bed, a family weeps.
Blinded by tears, they each recall past years.
She sees the angel's hand, she hears the soft command,
And one who reaches out with grandma's smiling eyes,
Leads her to the stairway of surprise.

DEATH

Death! A moving out of time
Into a realm where all belong,
A place of which few are aware,
Though all their loved ones linger there.
A place of learning and renewal,
Where each must meet himself and judge
His rights, his wrongs, his lies, his truth,
Where we all come to terms with destiny
Before we meet Love in eternity.

TIME

Time to put the memories away;

The year is ended on this winter day.

A year of love and laughter and despair,

A time of tears, of poetry and care.

ALONE

Old, unwanted, riches gone,
A hag, gaunt, aggressive, alone,
Living in the past. Not wanted by
this society; the sea to end it?
No courage; insomnia, despair;
Confused, defeated but not dead!
Is there no kindness, no Samaritan?
A smile, swift hope, fading,
No faith, no God, no hope.
Another smile, gone.
The sea? A voice, stay, help, apathy!
A hand offered, concerned eyes watching,
Warmth, a roof, hunger appeased.
Take me in, help me care.

FOR THOSE OF US WHO LOVED HIM

'Do not go gentle into that good night

Old age should burn and rave at close of day',*

So said the poet, as his father slept away.

Grief couldn't know the peacefulness of death,

Release from pain, release from loneliness,

A yielding of the burden, an easing of the struggle for each breath,

The heart that beats the rhythm of a lifetime simply lets go.

For those who watch with wonder, each demise,

Some will recall an earlier sacrifice,

A life of struggle or a life of joy.

This loss of ours did cheerfulness deploy,

A friendly word for all who came along,

For some, he made the world a brighter place,

Lit by the zany grin upon his face.

For those of us who loved him,

He gave, as parents do, the greatest gift-

He gave us life.

February 1991 Grandad Braund

*Do Not Go Gentle Into That Good Night
   - Dylan Thomas

THE DREAM

I dreamed I walked with death last night
Across a sunlit land.
There was no fear, there was no fright,
He took me gently by the hand,
And soft caressed my burning brow.
We walked a pleasant land.

I tossed, I turned in fevered sleep,
But rest eluded me,
Until that gentle presence came,
And peace I've searched for all my life,
So tenderly caressed me.

England's Grandmother

Born into history, somebody's child,
Lived through the crisis of war and still smiled.
Married to majesty; beauty and grace,
Always she showed us tranquillity's face.
A gentle example of humour and strength,
Both wife and mother, she went to great length
To learn to be Queen, to give faith, to inspire
A nation downhearted, depressed, and on fire.
War-torn and weary yet, thousands turned out
To see 'our Elizabeth' wave, and to shout.
Years passed and, like any family grown,
Saw the daughter she cherished succeed to the throne.
Sadness and sorrow serenely she met,
And shared with her people, no sign of regret.

THE PATH OF LOVE

Don't think, because I'm old and grey,

That love's old yearnings flown away.

I trace the path of love across the years

With memories of joy, despair and tears.

SADNESS

These eyes shall see no more the green fields that I love.
These nostrils shall not smell the fragrant blossom on the breeze.
This skin shall never feel again the soft caress of falling rain.
These ears shall fail to hear the dancing rustle of the trees.

Instead, eternal sleep will sweep the memories away.
The voice once filled with laughter will now in silence rest.
The heart that beat with vigour, fell in love, and filled with joy,
Will roam the plains of heaven in the soul's eternal quest,

HAIKU

Me, a statistic,
Waiting area crowded
Breast Clinic. Mrs. Braund?

SEPTICAEMIA

The Serpent bit. In
raging fires of fever,
I came to a place of angels,
And was healed.

ANOTHER

At the edge of dreams,
I soar on the wings of my soul.
Something within stirs.

WORK IN PROGRESS

The poison, at Oncologist's behest,
Like raspberry juice was dripping in my chest,
Through Hickman line, a serpent coiled upon my breast,
Holding at bay the errant cancer's quest.

Captive through our various treatments stages,
We sit, both genders, anxious or courageous.
Compassion flares, I've lived through man's seven ages
Seen my children's children turn life's pages.

Will she? Who holds her toddler on her knee;
Another watches, plays so quietly,
Sits at her feet. Head veiled like me,
She smiles, we share the waiting patiently.

GRANDMOTHER

The shadows on the cottage wall
Dance to the flickering flames,
Contented, the animals doze on the hearth,
As she tries to recall past names.
A succession of cats and dogs have slept
On a winter's night at her feet.
Family pets of a family long gone,
Leaving her life complete.

Alone with her memories, Grandmother sits
With her cat and her dog and her fire.
Summers and winters, autumns and springs,
Have fulfilled a lifetime's desire.
Frost at her window and snow at her door,
And fantasy flames on the wall,
Are all she has left, but she dreams with a smile
And waits for the end of it all.

AFTERWORD

AUTHOR'S NOTE

I am, in the widest sense, an autobiographical poet. I write about my own experiences, and have done since childhood; though most of the childhood scribblings are long gone. Those poems of childhood that remain; *Westward Ho!* and *Child of the Sea,* are true experiences if coloured by adult memory.

Childhood by the seashore was free of today's restrictions and fears, mine with a working mother and unremembered father was freer than most in the early 1950's. My playground was the cliffs, rocks, beaches and tors that bordered the North Devon village of Westward Ho!. In those days everyone knew everyone in the village and probably my every move was watched by someone, and reported to my mother if there was cause for concern. Like the day when the horse I was riding bolted through the village guided only by my small hands twisted in its mane; and the knees gripping tight as it raced round the corners, as I directed it to the long hill behind the church where I knew it must pull up. My friend Bubbles grazed the ponies on the burrows behind the Pebbleridge, the common land grazing which stretched for miles behind the golden sands. In the summer holidays I helped with the beach pony rides leading the ponies up and down for the visitors. I was paid in free rides! The ponies often scrambled over the pebbles to the beach in the early mornings making their way up the slipway invading the village. Bubbles was on yet another warning; control your ponies or lose your common grazing rights. I crept out at dawn as soon as I heard the clatter of hooves on the slipway, somehow clambered onto the rogue escapist and led the dozen or so ponies back to the burrows via quiet lanes before the village awoke. Fearful, I imagine, of losing my free rides!

Nursing, marriage and family life spawned many a verse, lost in time. A few remain. My personal quest for truth grew through the Anglican church into which I was confirmed at 19. Years later it was to delve deeply into the mystical approach of the major religions when I studied Psychology and Comparative Religion with the Open University.

Nursing started in a London hospital when I was 17 and spanned some 40 years in the NHS with a period in private work as our family grew up.

Like all nurses I saw much of death and healing. It became a specialist subject following a 6 week residential course at St Christopher's Hospice in Kent where I studied under Dame Cicely Saunders. It was here I found my professional teaching vocation leading to both clinical teaching and higher education; developing courses for professional nurses in death dying and bereavement for adults, children and their families.

Family life over three generations provided much inspiration, as did news events. *Death rides the Night Train* and *The News* came from the Taunton Train Crash and the Tenerife Air Crash.

When my daughter in law Henny became Chief Executive of the Anthony Nolan Trust and my son Mark ran his first marathon at fifty I sought to contribute also. The poem *Wanted* followed a conversation on how to encourage ethnic minorities to sign as donors. You will find it at the front of this collection from which all proceeds will go to the Anthony Nolan Trust for that work which has already saved so many lives.

    I have included footnotes where a poem seems to need it. Most are self evident.

Jeni Braund 2016. Devon

Made in the USA
Charleston, SC
12 November 2016